3—

D0975175

Following
Sound into
SILENCE

Hay House Titles of Related Interest

THE ASTONISHING POWER OF EMOTIONS: Let Your Feelings Be Your Guide,
by Esther and Jerry Hicks (The Teachings of Abraham™)

CHANGE YOUR THOUGHTS—CHANGE YOUR LIFE:
Living the Wisdom of the Tao,
by Dr. Wayne W. Dyer

CHOICES AND ILLUSIONS: How Did I Get Where I Am,
and How Do I Get Where I Want to Be?,
by Eldon Taylor

CREATING INNER HARMONY: Using Your Voice and Music to Heal,
by Don Campbell (book-with-CD)

THE GOLDEN COMPASS: What Is Spiritual Guidance?
by Joan Z. Borysenko, Ph.D., and Gordon Franklin Dveirin, Ed.D.

THE JOURNEY TO THE SACRED GARDEN:
A Guide to Traveling in the Spiritual Realms,
by Hank Wesselman, Ph.D. (book-with-CD)

LOVE YOUR VOICE: Use Your Speaking Voice to Create Success,
Self-Confidence, and Star-like Charisma!,
by Roger Love (book-with-CD)

THE POWER OF PLEASURE: Maximizing Your Enjoyment for a Lifetime,
by Douglas Weiss, Ph.D.

All of the above are available at your local bookstore,
or may be ordered by visiting:

Hay House USA: www.hayhouse.com®
Hay House Australia: www.hayhouse.com.au
Hay House UK: www.hayhouse.co.uk
Hay House South Africa: www.hayhouse.co.za
Hay House India: www.hayhouse.co.in

Following Sound into SILENCE

Chanting Your Way Beyond Ego into Bliss

Kailash
(Kurt A. Bruder, Ph.D., M.Ed.)

HAY HOUSE, INC.
Carlsbad, California • New York City
London • Sydney • Johannesburg
Vancouver • Hong Kong • New Delhi

Published and distributed in the United States by: Hay House, Inc.: www.
hayhouse.com • *Published and distributed in Australia by:* Hay House
Australia Pty. Ltd.: www.hayhouse.com.au • *Published and distributed in the
United Kingdom by:* Hay House UK, Ltd.: www.hayhouse.co.uk • *Published
and distributed in the Republic of South Africa by:* Hay House SA (Pty), Ltd.:
www.hayhouse.co.za • *Distributed in Canada by:* Raincoast: www.raincoast.
com • *Published in India by:* Hay House India: www.hayhouse.co.in

Editorial supervision: Jill Kramer • *Design:* Amy Rose Grigoriou
Illustrations: Kurt A. Bruder (Kailash); *Interior photos:* **www.shutterstock.
com**; Kurt A. Bruder (Kailash); **www.jiunlimited.com**; Grigory Kubatyan •
Font dingbats design courtesy of: **www.dafont.com** and **www.aenigmafonts.
com**

Library of Congress Control Number: 2006940286

ISBN: 978-1-4019-1678-7

11   10   09   08   4   3   2   1
1st edition, January 2008

Printed in China

Contents

Introduction

Invitation to Chanting

Are you hoping to find a simple, straightforward spiritual practice that reliably calms and concentrates your mind, elevates and stabilizes your feelings, and inspires and energizes your will?

The fact that you're reading this book suggests that you're already a spiritual seeker—someone wanting to experience the Great Mystery directly and hoping that this experience will translate into concrete improvements in your day-to-day life. Devotional chanting is the very spiritual practice you need, allowing you to take full advantage of a resource that's already available to you for your own evolution: your voice.

If you're like me, at some time or another you've been inspired by stories of saints and sages. You've probably imagined yourself becoming like them—holy, compassionate, wise, and carefree—only to discover that wishing didn't take you there. Learning about how great someone else's spiritual life was doesn't do much by itself to improve your own. True enough, reading about their heroic efforts with respect to self-discipline and their amazing insights can be inspiring. However, it can also be discouraging in the long run, especially when you discover that the particulars of their path are simply too ambitious for you to imitate.

Yet, there's this nagging sense that you can be more than you've been thus far and that a way of life that transcends your current limitations exists, if only you knew how to access it. But where do you begin?

What you need is a system for spiritual development that works with your life as it is, yet challenges you enough to result in definite growth. It should stretch you where you need to expand and provide incentive to strive where you've been lax, while not overwhelming you with its complexity or difficulty. The practical spiritual exercise of devotional chanting has filled these needs for me, and I know it can do the same for you.

My own entry into chanting was from two different "angles." One was my search for an approach to spiritual growth that would engage every dimension of my being, especially my feelings. For many years, my emphasis was on cultivating the clearest and most accurate understanding of ultimate reality that I could. This process led me to consider a wide variety of perspectives, first exclusively within Christianity, and then within other wisdom traditions as well. While I learned many things that I still regard as valuable, this philosophical approach was sometimes rather "dry" and detached. I wanted a practice that involved all of me—my body and heart, as well as my mind—which would lead me to a direct experience of the ideals I was pursuing. Devotional chanting delivers.

The other point of entry for me was my work as a scholar-teacher of communication. For the bulk of my professional life, I've been investigating the relationship between people's specific communication behaviors and their interior lives, especially their sense of self. I came to realize that everything we say (or sing) to ourselves and others shapes us and contributes to the quality of our lives. My studies of interactive methods for spiritual development that have been used by people throughout history and around the world inevitably led me to devotional chanting.

In 2002, I was fortunate to find my guru, Bhagavan Das. There's no one in the Western world who has done more to promote devotional chanting than this extraordinary man. Since then, under his guidance and following his example, I've been leading chanting events and offering spiritual instruction across North America. Every day I learn more about how chanting works, and my appreciation of its power and sophistication as a procedure for promoting well-being, happiness, and transcendence continues to grow. My goal is to make what I've learned about this ideal form of communication—in both my secular and spiritual training—available to as many people as I can.

Why Chant?

The advantages of this ancient form of worshipping the Divine are many and varied. Not only does chanting quiet our minds, it also helps us forget our troubles; produces a sense of connection with others; and fosters a wealth of positive feelings such as serenity, lightness, and joy. Many chanters—novices and veterans alike—even report the sensation of having transcended their bodies during this practice. Chanting is a technique that makes the best use of our love of pleasure, redirecting our desires toward the Supreme. In this way, chanting is a shortcut to ecstasy.

Mantra repetition is a simple, enjoyable, and powerful procedure for purposefully reorganizing your consciousness. The uncomplicated nature of chanting may seem at odds with some of the extravagant claims made for its power as a form of spiritual technology. After all, how could speaking or singing syllables from an ancient foreign language possibly generate such an amazing range of benefits? As you'll see, the very act of repeating a mantra induces relaxation, allowing you access to the sublime silence always abiding at the core of your being. Simplifying your mental processes by working with mantras will support you in increased concentration and emotional command.

Additional benefits may be realized when you chant in coordination with other types of *sadhana* (spiritual practice). For example, the rewards of chanting are exponentially increased when also harnessing the force of imagination—such as repeating mantras while visualizing the Perfections that are being invoked. (Throughout this book I'll be using the term *Perfection* to mean the Supreme in any form whatsoever, personified or otherwise.) As you move through these pages, you'll learn about other benefits common to all mantras, as well as many that are linked to the repetition of specific mantras.

In the first chapter, we'll look at how chanting shows up across times and places, and we'll confront the tendency toward religious bigotry—an attitude that can prevent people from taking full advantage of the possibilities available to them in devotional chanting. Then we'll explore the essential ingredients of chanting in the second chapter.

Chapter 3 examines how chanting supports a healthy mental life and identity, including how it can help you control your thoughts, quiet your mind, and realize your ideals. Chapter 4 addresses the way relating with devotion to the Perfections invoked in mantras impacts your feelings. You'll discover how chanting reorganizes your attachments, how its beauty elevates your life experience. As a remarkably effective emotional yoga, this practice will help you identify with what's best and highest within you.

You'll delve into the communal dimension of chanting in Chapter 5, looking first at the way seemingly separate individuals are shaped by the communities that they belong to. Chanting with a group can dramatically extend the transformative potential of this practice beyond the scope of solitary chanting. It will help you recognize just how deeply you're connected with others and how potent these bonds are in fashioning your life. It may even motivate you to be more selective about those you attach yourself to.

Supported by the companion CD to this book, you can begin or expand your chanting practice. There are 14 carefully chosen mantras in Chapter 6 (and another in the Conclusion) that, if approached with devotion, will take you to bliss. In the Conclusion, you'll see how chanting can be a vital part of a practice for furthering your happiness and growth. You'll be empowered to use devotional chanting as a means to recognize the sacred in everything.

As you move through this material, you'll be encouraged to follow the sound of your own voice into the pristine silence that permanently abides in your heart-center. It's reassuring to realize that no matter how crazy the world gets or how great the pressures and distractions are within you, you have a remedy that's never farther away than your own voice.

Applying What You Learn

Throughout this book, you'll be invited to apply certain concepts and practices. Just as reading a doctor's prescription isn't a substitute for taking the medicine, getting the full benefit of these ideas and methods is impossible without putting them into practice.

We've all had our fill of learning that never progressed beyond the level of mere concepts. The only wisdom that counts, that actually benefits us, is that which we embody in our behavior; the rest is, at best, potential knowledge. This is especially true in the case of procedures for spiritual development. A method for personal growth that doesn't find its way into concrete action is a path not taken, and it will result in little or no transformation in our lives. And transformation is what we're striving for . . . so we can finally lead the Divine life that is our birthright.

So go ahead—have some fun challenging yourself with this exciting and enjoyable approach to advancing your evolution. As you read through the text, you'll encounter opportunities to reflect on your experience and suggestions for actions you can take to put these ideas and skills to work for you.

Happy chanting!

Chapter One

Clearing Your Way to Chant

Chanting Across Traditions

The word *chant* comes from the Latin *cantare,* "to sing." Of course, chanting is more than merely singing. It's using your powers of vocalization and hearing to directly experience and unite with the Great Mystery in sound form. Repeating sacred sounds drives their vibrations deep into your mind and heart, eventually taking you from where you are to where you want to be.

Most systems of spiritual practice—Eastern and Western, ancient and contemporary—employ some form of chanting in their repertoire of techniques for connecting with the sacred. Speaking certain words that describe and honor your highest ideals puts you in touch with a quality of life beyond ordinary experience. Repeating such words with sufficient focus and emotional intensity will help you bridge the gap between you and the Divine.

Wherever and whenever you look, you find people repeating the names and praises of the Supreme. For instance, although the ancient Israelites treated the revealed name of God with such reverence that they would never speak it aloud, they were no strangers to repeating *Hashem* (Hebrew for "the Name"); they substituted a host of honorifics in its place (including Lord, Most High, Holy One, Our Father and King, and Shepherd of Israel). Christians routinely refer to Jesus Christ by a variety of titles (such as God with Us, Lion of Judah, King of Kings, Prince of Peace, and Lamb of God). Muslims celebrate the 99 beautiful names of Allah (such as the Merciful, Granter of Security, Protector, Forgiver, and the Truth), each paying tribute to a different attribute of the Divine.

Despite Buddhists' nontheistic orientation, it's a common practice for them to remember both the historical Buddha and a great many other awakened beings and *yidams* (meditation deities) through the recitation of their names and praises. Among Sikhs, many names of the Divine are featured in hymns and mantras from their scripture, the Guru Granth Sahib. These are regularly chanted to turn the mind toward

2

God and the teaching of their Ten Gurus ("removers of darkness"). Such examples may be multiplied indefinitely across traditions.

Turn your mind toward your own upbringing. You can probably recall times when you repeated words that expressed sacred sentiments, whether during Sunday-school activities, in bedtime prayers, or while celebrating religious holidays—perhaps singing Christmas carols, participating in a Passover seder, or taking part in some other festival. These are all practices related to devotional chanting.

While there have been a great variety of texts, languages, melodies, and cultural customs associated with chanting throughout human history and around the world, my primary focus will be on chanting practices based in Sanskrit—an ancient Indian language developed specifically to support spiritual inquiry, exercise, and achievement. I heartily acknowledge the enormous value of other approaches to chanting and continue to benefit from them in my own personal practice. Indeed, most of what I have to say about Sanskrit chanting is applicable to other traditions. But since my own study and experience is anchored in the Sanskrit-based variety, for the purposes of this book I emphasize the methods and understandings that have arisen within it. I leave it to you to explore the similarities and differences between this and other chanting traditions as you see fit.

My Own Chanting Background

My first experience with chanting was the repetition of the Jesus Prayer ("Lord Jesus Christ, Son of God, have mercy on me") in the early 1990s. This is a venerable practice of *hesychast* (Greek for "silence" or "stillness") spirituality within Eastern Orthodox Christianity. I was spending a great deal of time at a small monastery in central Texas doing fieldwork for my doctoral dissertation—a close examination of communication among the monks and nuns. I was also relating to them as spiritual family members since I'd converted to Orthodoxy a few years before.

Under the direction of a seasoned monk, I repeated this prayer daily for long intervals. I coordinated the repetitions with my breathing, counting them on my *chotki* (a knotted-cord rosary), while I visualized Jesus hearing me. I did this during times specifically set aside for prayer and also when I found a free moment between other activities—while driving, for example, or on an airplane. Over time, these words and thoughts of Christ permeated my mind. I was surprised to discover that the prayer seemed to be echoing in my mind at all times, often just below the threshold of my awareness, and I could chant along with it when I wished to.

Given my background in conservative Protestantism (famously uncomfortable with formal ritual and liturgy), I was initially concerned about the apparent incompatibility of this practice with Jesus's dictum "But when ye pray, use not vain repetitions, as the heathen do: for they think that they shall be heard for their much speaking" (Matthew 6:7). However, I soon realized that my use of repetition was not "vain." Mine wasn't a hollow or selfish act; it was occasioned by sincere devotion to God. Nor did my attempt to attract God's ear come through increasing the sheer quantity of my words; rather, I understood that repeating this prayer was about cultivating positive changes in my mind and heart.

In the years since, I've incorporated concepts and practices from many of the world's wisdom traditions. I've retained my appreciation for that early chanting experience and my devotion to Jesus Christ and his teachings—even though I no longer identify exclusively with Christianity. So it was with considerable sympathy and understanding that I listened to a participant at a Sanskrit chanting event as she revealed, with obvious discomfort, a grave concern: She loved to chant, but having been raised in a Christian church (her father was a pastor), she was terrified that she might go to hell if she continued. Given the cultural dominance of Christianity in North America, it's possible that you share this anxiety. You might be worried that chanting the names and praises of ideals from another place, time, and language may be spiritually harmful. I hope to put any such concerns to rest so that you can approach devotional chanting without fear.

Tackling Religious Chauvinism

Because of our minds' limits, we can never comprehend God. Everyone's notions of the Divine are partial, emphasizing certain aspects of the Supreme that are understood to be essential, while excluding others. Our emphases typically correspond to the concept of Divinity that we've inherited as a member of a particular family and faith community. Treating our own religious legacy as the one and only truth for all people and times may provide a reassuring sense of certainty, but it requires that we dismiss as mistaken any idea, value, or practice that has its origin outside of the narrow confines of our inherited belief system.

Human beings have been asking the big questions for a very long time: *Who am I? Why am I here? Where did I and everything else come from? How can I live in order to be happy?* In earnestly attempting to answer these questions, we've accumulated a great storehouse of wisdom. But because most of the solutions differ from what we're used to, we may mistake much of this treasure for rubbish. The answers that we find acceptable and those we're likely to reject are matters that are usually decided very early in our life experience following a simple rubric: The familiar is good; the strange is bad. We define ourselves with reference to that tiny portion of the universe we find ourselves attached to through routine exposure. And we often do this without any conscious choice. This is the basis for our feelings of sympathy for some answers and our indifference or even hatred toward others.

Recall times when you've reacted judgmentally to other people's religious beliefs and practices just because they were different from your own. This kind of bias is commonplace and may escape your notice—unless you happen to be on the receiving end of it. Have you ever been judged harshly in this way? How did it make you feel?

We tend to react fearfully to the unknown—the foreign and unfamiliar. This is an automatic, defensive reaction that proves helpful to us much of the time, since it maintains the comfortable, safe status quo of our lives, shielding us from potential dangers. After all, when we're in strange surroundings, we don't know our way; without a sense of the "rules" in a given situation, it's easy to make a costly mistake. But in the matter of spirituality as elsewhere, excluding any particular idea or approach just because it's different from what we're used to is a kind of prejudice. It cuts us off not merely from others who are unlike us, but also from all their answers to those perennial questions that human beings face.

8

Every concept of the Divine most likely has some merit; it probably conveys valuable intuitive information regarding ultimate reality. But no description of the Supreme is exhaustive. Our limited minds can't comprehend infinity, and every effort to grasp Deity involves abstraction (a process that leaves some things out, while privileging others); reification (treating complex, subtle features of reality as if they were simple, concrete things); and analogy (understanding one thing in terms of another). Your picture of the Divine is surely different from mine, but that doesn't mean that either of us is incorrect—just that each image is anchored in, and conditioned by, our respective personal and cultural histories.

Our tendency is to approach spiritual exercises such as devotional chanting within the boundaries of our customary, familiar religious tradition—and that's a terrific place to start. We can cultivate our spiritual abilities through devotion to whatever form of the Divine is most inspiring to us. As our capacity for concentration and care grow through practice, we may discover that other people's ideas are also valuable. Although these portraits of Deity may initially seem foreign, or even to be false gods or goddesses, they too are the fruit of honest efforts to glimpse Perfection, just like our familiar conceptions. This is a Perfection that's so vast and inconceivable that many forms and names are required even to hint at its many-faceted excellence. Indeed, as we've seen, even those who believe in a single, almighty Creator (as in the great monotheisms—Judaism, Christianity, and Islam) address, praise, and describe the Divine using many names, each of which captures a distinct dimension of Deity.

Every sincere answer to the perennial questions humans face is valuable. Each offers insight not only into the Great Mystery itself, but into the history and values of the very people who are asking the questions. We all have ideas about the "shape" of ultimate reality—some conceptions are more fluid, others are more fixed; some are clearer, others are more ambiguous; some are more complex, others are less elaborate. Our notions reveal something about our own development. Each of us has an impression of what Perfection must be like, and that sense is likely to be expressed in a manner that's consistent with our experience and interests.

Our ordinary way of experiencing the world is dualistic: We see ourselves as distinct from whatever we encounter through our perceptions and in our thoughts. Even our ideal is visualized (at least initially) as distinct from ourselves. Since our concept of the Supreme has been forged in the context of relationship with other human beings, it's not surprising that we tend to understand the infinite in the familiar, finite terms of individuals in relationship.

Close your eyes for a moment and imagine how a deity of, say, peace might appear. Chances are that when you're finished, you probably will have assigned a gender, certain physical attributes, accessories, attitudes, and personality features to this figure.

Conceived in this way, the Divine occurs to us like a human being, albeit greatly magnified and considerably less limited.

With a steadfast spiritual exercise such as devotional chanting, we may realize that these personified Perfections are transcendent dimensions of our own highest selves. But at first it's easier for us to get our heads around the infinite if we imagine it in the more manageable proportions of a finite form, described in words or rendered in some artistic medium.

We may suppose that our notion of the Divine is complete, but when we honestly review our efforts, the partial character of the labels and images we've used becomes obvious. Every effort to express the inexpressible must fall short of its goal. It's dangerous when we mistake our limited *portrayals* of the Divine for God—as if mere words or pictures could contain the Supreme. We can actually hinder our spiritual growth if we suppose that our depiction of the infinite is sufficient. This prideful perspective calls a halt to learning, since we're satisfied that we already possess the ultimate answer.

A stubborn insistence that ours is the only legitimate portrayal of the Supreme is another closely related hazard. When we're convinced of the exclusivity of our grasp on God, we're unlikely to extend compassion—the genuine measure of authentic spiritual maturity—to those whose concepts differ from our own.

Taking Up the Name

Thankfully, it's possible for you to approach the Divine through your favored names and forms while acknowledging their essentially limited character. This empowers you to graciously accept the variety of representations of Deity, confident that all images of Perfection can elevate your soul toward its own limitless potential, even though the symbols you may use are limited.

Your encounter with Perfection inevitably occurs within your imagination; indeed, where else could such a meeting occur? The human mind is very powerful, capable of containing (on a conceptual level) all space and time and everything occurring within them. As you stretch your imagination by developing increasingly vast and multifaceted understandings of the Supreme, you're changed in the process. What you imagine has real repercussions for your life. You're being shaped right now by your concept of the Divine, whatever that may be. For starters, it's influencing your idea of your own highest self.

When you chant, you extol the praises of the Supreme across as many names and forms of the Divine as you can sincerely embrace with your heart. As I mentioned before, no quantity of depictions or descriptions can ever exhaust the

12

glories of the Absolute. I believe that you needn't be concerned that Divinity will be angry or threatened over your using the "wrong" name or form. Rest easy—God knows God's name.

All names and forms of God suggest, at best, some few facets of a splendor so incalculable as to outstrip all attempts to represent it in language and art. Your task is to take up one or more of these names—from any tradition that touches your heart—and repeat it (or them) with devotion, reminding yourself continually of the source of life, love, and light.

You'd do well to guard your heart against an attitude of superiority, in chanting as elsewhere. No particular language, lyric, tune, or form of the Divine will suit all paths, tastes, and dispositions. Giving yourself (and others) the space to discover and pursue the style of chanting that's most pleasing and helpful, while remaining open to learning from others, may prove to be the most rewarding approach for all.

Sensitized to your own potential for religious narrow-mindedness, you can now explore previously unfamiliar spiritual methods with a greater likelihood of success—beginning with devotional chanting and its essential ingredients: voice, mantra, and song.

Chapter Two

Voice, Mantra, and Song: The Raw Material of Chanting

Voice: A Tool for Directing Your Consciousness

Chanting, in one form or another, has always been vital to humans. It's a practice that fosters our experience of transcendence, spurring us to go beyond ourselves. Our unique capacity for self-awareness (and, therefore, spiritual depth) is rooted in our unequaled ability to intelligently manipulate vocal sound. Harnessing this power is crucial, because we're much more vulnerable to auditory information than we are to other modes of perception. We have lids on our eyes, not on our ears, so being selective about the sounds we expose ourselves to requires some effort. Whatever the origin or quality, everything we experience influences our consciousness. Some encounters support our peace, health, and development; others don't. Chanting provides a greater measure of control over our sound inputs—and therefore over our thoughts and feelings.

We share a profound intuitive wonder at vocal sound with both our ancestors and our contemporaries. Isn't it amazing that we can convey intricate ideas, plumb the depths of our hearts, and coordinate our actions just by making noises? Even the most no-nonsense examination of speech reveals a power bordering on the magical. Every aspect of human beings—our physiology, psychology, sociology, and spirituality—has evolved as a living system in which vocalization and hearing play a central role. It's not overstating matters to say that our consciousness is hardwired to follow where our voices lead it.

Voice is a tool for selectively directing awareness. It permits you to symbolically represent objects—from tangible matter to the most refined idea of the Supreme—to yourself and others. As a human being, you're defined by your ability to produce and interpret vocalized sound meaningfully. In other words, you're uniquely equipped to make noises with your voice that you and other listeners take to *mean* certain things.

The babbling of infants is rewarded by their parents and in time crystallizes into recognizable names for objects (for example, *kitty* and *doggy*). This ability, enhanced over years

of development, permits thought, discussion, and coopera-
tive action regarding the most complex and abstract concepts
imaginable—veterinary medicine, for instance, or the clichéd
question of whether dogs have "Buddha nature" (that is, are
nonhuman sentient beings also essentially Radiant Awareness
and Care?). The greatest feats of humanity are initiated, organized, coordinated, and executed in and through language.

But it all starts with the association of certain patterns of
vocalized sound with particular features of the world. Whether it's children learning their first words or adults acquiring a
second tongue, repeated references to a given object or action
using the same cluster of vocal sounds solidifies an impression
that these syllables are the name—the sonic counterpart—of
that object or action. Our continual labeling stabilizes the
whirling flux of the world into mentally manageable fragments and relationships between those fragments. A given
label may then be used to conjure up what it stands for in the
mind of the speaker and hearer even in the absence of that
object or action.

We remain forever fascinated by the sound of our own
voices (even as I write this, my infant son Bodhi is squealing
with delight, apparently celebrating nothing more than his
ability to make powerful noises). We're positively magnetized

to speech and song, and barring some hindrance, we *will* talk and sing—if only to try to convince ourselves of our own existence. We correctly intuit the importance of speech. We know in our hearts that our lives and worlds are shaped by what we say, even though we frequently dilute our sacred potential with trivial chitchat, small talk, and self-absorbed rambling or distort it with gossip, deception, and self-abuse.

Why don't you try monitoring your talk over a couple of hours today, keeping a record of what you say.

- How much of it is positive and negative?
- True and false?
- Were there any wasted words?

18

Chanting provides a constructive alternative to this commonplace waste and injury. It gives us something ultimately useful to say beyond the chatter that all too often occupies our mouths and minds. If we say and sing better things to ourselves, perhaps we may think, feel, and *be* better for it.

We feed our physical bodies by taking the energy of food in through our mouths. The subtler aspects of our being are nourished—or starved or poisoned—by what comes *out* of our mouths. Repeating mantras is an accessible practice that optimizes our speech, allowing us to reap the best fruit that our mouths can produce. Our speech must be purified and made worthwhile if we're to truly discover and realize our full potential.

Mantra: Invocation of Perfection

The origin of the word *mantra* is uncertain. Some say that it means "mind protector," from the Sanskrit *manas* (mind) + *tram* (protector). Others argue that its meaning is "instrument of thought," *man* (to think) + *tra* (tool). Both possible origins suggest that mantras are specialized verbal tools for directing our thoughts along particular, beneficial pathways, resulting in the dramatic reduction of the sheer quantity of thoughts and—more specifically—the exclusion of those that are harmful.

19

Unfortunately, the concept has become diluted in the popular mind-set and the media, resulting in a widespread misunderstanding of, and lack of appreciation for, what mantras genuinely offer. In common usage, a *mantra* is a word or phrase that you repeat to yourself, at least mentally, similar to an affirmation. Repetition is an important factor in working with mantras, but there's much more to realizing their potential than merely multiplying the number of times that you speak them.

Think about how you may have already used the concept of mantras:

- Have you ever repeated a word or phrase to yourself?

- What did you hope would happen— and what was the result?

The power of real mantras is based on the fact that words conjure up entire worlds in speakers' minds; they make what's named symbolically present. Mantras invoke Perfection. Most name and express homage to a particular deity; they summon and announce Perfection in personified form. For instance, AUM NAMO HANUMATAY HUNG heralds the arrival of Hanuman (depicted on page 22), the monkey god whose incomparable devotion and might are celebrated in the Indian epic the *Ramayana*. Others, AUM AH HUNG, for example, describe—however cryptically—some ultimately desirable state of affairs, such as the attainment of enlightenment (or, in this case, the purification of body, speech, and mind).

AUM AH HUNG
in Tibetan script.

These sorts of mantras are very like affirmations, except that they're expressed in Sanskrit and many times in a highly condensed form (an example being my effort to interpret the Six-Syllable Mantra, the seventh in Chapter 6!). Some are so condensed, in fact, that you'd need special instruction from a qualified teacher in order to recite them with understanding. However, your dedicated repetition will usually assist you in achieving the revolution in consciousness prescribed by the particular mantra. Each mantra embodies the very Perfection that it stands for in acoustic form, epitomizing an ideal your consciousness may arrive at over time

Hanuman

through devotional exercise and identification. As you work with it, you align your awareness with a palpable sound current that directly corresponds to the Perfection it expresses.

Perspectives on Mantras

There are a variety of perspectives people take when working with mantras. Some approach them as magical spells with which they directly manipulate the world. Others view them as sacred phrases that can be used to request the aid of supernatural beings. Still others regard them as the product of ancient poetic efforts—artists expressing their ideals and bringing order to their world through the precise aesthetic arrangement of speech sounds.

The most widely accepted traditional belief about Sanskrit mantras (and Sanskrit in general) is expressed in mythology. It's a tale of extraordinary beings, *rishis* (seers), who engaged in extreme meditation for eons before the creation of the physical universe. In a state of profound contemplative absorption, they heard the *bīja* (seed syllables), the individual speech sounds of Sanskrit, gaining direct knowledge of their corresponding energies or qualities. The syllables were combined to form the Vedas, the most ancient scriptures in the world, held to be the result of revelation rather than the product of human invention. These sounds are understood to possess creative power, such that speaking them under the right conditions creates the very reality that they represent.

From this perspective, there's an essential (that is, inherent) connection between specific sound patterns in Sanskrit mantras and their meanings, their effects in the world. In many passages in the Hindu scriptures, these sounds are depicted as carrying and conveying supernatural energy, sometimes even in the absence of any faith or piety on the part of the person uttering them.

The mythic account of mantras' power is problematic for someone like me, a conscientious scientist trained to accept only those claims that can be verified by hard data. People subscribing to this belief take the traditional account as historical fact, without direct knowledge or confirming evidence. But as you'll soon see, you don't need to accept the legendary origin of Sanskrit to conclude that there's a very real and powerful connection between the sounds that compose mantras and their corresponding Perfections.

There are various words for the same thing or process across different languages. For example, the English word *dog* refers to the same thing as the French word *chien*. This suggests that the link between sound and meaning is arbitrary; there's no essential (and, therefore, no universal) connection between any specific pattern of vocalization and what it names. This observation applies to Sanskrit as much as to any other language. However, prolonged widespread usage of a given pattern in connection with a distinct meaning usually results in a strong impression that there's a natural, even necessary, link between the sounds and some specific meaning.

Particular vocal sounds are sometimes so closely associated with certain kinds of experience that they seem inherently bound together. The pairings are so consistent that we might suppose these sounds and what they stand for to be linked in a nonarbitrary way. For instance, *Ah* expresses relief and satisfaction; a drawn-out *M* implies some form of sensual pleasure; *Sh* is widely used when requesting silence. Can you think of any other speech sounds that seem to have an essential or universal meaning?

Such examples fall well short of the contention that the sound elements of Sanskrit (or any other human language) are intrinsically meaningful apart from conventional agreement among speakers over time. Usually, we simply inherit established pairings of sound and meaning as we learn a given language.

The practice of chanting Sanskrit mantras is among history's greatest examples of an applied remedy for psychological suffering. It's been in continual operation for millennia and has spread over the bulk of the globe, testing the impact of channeling the human mind in precise therapeutic directions through the use of specific verbal prescriptions. The precision, regularity, and devotion with which the mantras have been transmitted throughout the ages have helped foster the impression that specific sound patterns are joined to certain effects. This connection is archetypal in scope and potency, influencing the individual and collective consciousness of spiritual practitioners across several of the world's major religions—most obviously among Hindus, Buddhists, Sikhs, and Jains.

We're living in the midst of a massive cultural—and especially religious—exchange between the East and the West. This began seriously in the last century; was spurred by advances in transportation, communication, and information processing; and was aided by shifting geopolitics. As a result, Sanskrit-based chanting is now following in the footsteps of its widespread familiar cousin, *hatha yoga*. Several spiritual systems recommending mantra repetition, together with a supernatural view of how these sounds function, have made their way into the West.

To discover the full power of mantras, I'm convinced that we'll need to delve beyond a mythic perspective that their effectiveness is based on the inherent force of the sounds that compose them. They aren't magical formulas intrinsically invested with supernatural powers or virtue (although many people, even great saints and sages, have treated them as if they were). Rather, mantras serve as sonic representations of varying facets of an enlightened condition that—while producing effects in the physical world and the less tangible realm of the mind and culture—has its origin in the subtlest realm of Spirit (a concept that will be developed further in this book). Mantras afford access to transcendental dimensions of our own being.

Although mantras may seem to be merely words or vocal sounds, they aren't the product of linguistic skill or mental prowess. Their potential as spiritual tools can't be accounted for entirely within that domain. They're instruments for human progress beyond the limits of language and the symbol-driven mind. To speak with authority about the meaning of any mantra, you must first actualize its potential by sincerely and steadfastly repeating it with devotion . . . only then can you ascertain its meaning for yourself. Discovering this isn't a matter of merely translating and defining words; you could do that and remain untouched. Rather, by making your thoughts and feelings reverberate with these sounds, you gradually come to resemble the very Perfection accessed through them.

Enlightenment, the source and goal of mantras, is your innate nature—in fact, Radiant Awareness and Care is the foundation of your very being. But it has become obscured through misunderstandings about who and what you are. Through a consistent, devoted chanting practice, you can cultivate mental and emotional routines that amount to a total internal makeover. False notions and unworkable habits are stripped away, rendering you more focused, balanced, peaceful, creative, loving, wise, self-possessed, and blissful than you were previously. Your investment in dedicated spiritual exercise can transform you to such an extent that some onlookers might get the impression that you have access to magical spells and the powers they bestow.

A mythic perspective on mantras can be particularly appealing to people who greedily desire power and instant gratification. Such individuals wish to avoid the hard work and self-sacrifice involved in realizing the promise of any procedure for transformation, devotional chanting included. Those who are attracted to spiritual quick fixes—narcissistic religious dabblers, spiritual materialists, New Age tourists, and the like—are typically on the lookout for the next religious "thing." They like the idea that they can harness the force of a mantra without jeopardizing their self-centered tendencies.

But real growth is the product of a significant reorganization of your mental, emotional, behavioral, and relational habits over time. As you'll soon see, while there are no short-cuts to lasting, beneficial change, there are many factors that contribute greatly to genuine spiritual development through devotional chanting.

Song: Giving Wings to Your Mantra

Your experience of positive transformation is greatly encouraged by the skillful combination of words with music. Typically, you begin working with a mantra by speaking it. Although many of the benefits associated with this practice are attainable through unadorned, spoken (and even silent, mental) repetition, singing mantras will enhance your rewards. Doing so allows you to exploit the power of music to stimulate intense positive emotion, embed material deeply and enduringly into your consciousness, and facilitate the feeling of connection with like-minded people.

When engaging in *japam* (spoken mantra repetition), what starts out as an awkward effort to articulate unfamiliar syllables becomes, with time and dedication, a graceful current that seems to arise all by itself. With sufficient repetition—and the consistency of sound that this makes possible—even spoken mantras tend to take on a tuneful quality. Nearly all of those I've set to music emerged out of long periods of speaking them. The way that I uttered each mantra settled into a certain rhythmic and melodic pattern that supported me in a condition of concentrated devotion.

For example, I'd been working with the mantra KARMAPA CHENNO (Track 12 on the accompanying CD), speaking it aloud and mentally rehearsing it. I'd been chewing on these syllables for several months when the way that I now chant it suddenly occurred to me, fully formed, seemingly out of nowhere. The simple meter and melody lends itself to extended periods of effortless repetition. Here, as with other mantras, the musical dimension of chanting introduces qualities into the experience that aren't available by simply speaking it.

First and foremost, the intense, worshipful feeling that's the hallmark of devotion is amplified by the marriage of mantra and music. Is there anything that arouses and shapes your emotions as powerfully and consistently as music? Try the following exercise:

1.   Watch your favorite movie and pay special attention to how the music influences your feelings.

2.   Consider this question: Do you think that you'd be having the same sort of viewing experience if the soundtrack were absent?

Music's emotionally evocative potential makes it ideal for a devotional approach to spirituality—one where you cultivate the strongest possible feelings of love for your ideal as a direct experience of the Divine. It's likely that you already have some music that you can count on to help you relax, along with tunes that you find inspiring or exciting and some that you perceive as romantic. When you chant, you're trying to cultivate each of these qualities (and others), although the emotions generated may shift at various points during your practice.

Even with only modest exposure to Sanskrit chanting, you'll notice that a given mantra may be set to a wondrous variety of music. You've probably observed different tunes used even within a single chant. These coordinate with the varying moods, as well as different levels of emotional intensity, that the singer is cultivating in the moment. You can experience this intensity by chanting with a full voice and holding a clear intention to feel as deeply as possible for the Perfection you're celebrating. The dynamic range of feeling is created by noticeable contrasts between the musical-emotional quality of one segment and another within the larger structure of the chant. For example, energetic, forceful, triumphant elements characterizing one passage are juxtaposed with a sequence that feels more gentle and subtle, with a quality of yearning. It's not so much that any particular phrase has these qualities in itself; rather, the marked musical shift (of a given phrase in relation to its predecessor) evokes the desired elevation of feeling.

Directing your emotions along an intensely loving trajectory is crucial when chanting mantras. This experience is fostered by a series of arcs of increasing musical intensity. Using your vocal and listening skills to ride these waves consolidates your attention and affection, resulting in mental and emotional purification as extraneous thoughts and feelings fall away.

Choosing Your Music

Some folks recommend using only certain traditional melodies in chanting, while others advocate setting mantras to contemporary tunes. Given these differences in taste, I believe that we should extend each other a great deal of latitude regarding the music we choose. As long as your choice supports you in sincere, sustained worship, it's a good one. That said, through careful analysis and many centuries of practical trial, the wisdom traditions have arrived at proven ways to guide the mind and heart to a condition of focus and bliss.

Therefore, time-honored music shouldn't be ignored or lightly abandoned.

We can observe a great deal of variation in the musical structure employed across different traditions of chanting. Sometimes even chant leaders in the same school of thought may make very different musical choices. The approach that I use is modeled on what I've learned from my guru, who studied among *sādhus* (men whose vocation is spiritual practice) in the Himalayan region of India.

In this tradition, group chanting takes a somewhat predictable form. Individual chants, regardless of their lyrics, often begin at a relatively low volume, slow tempo (sometimes ponderously slow to allow those who are less experienced to acquaint themselves with the simple lyrics), and limited range of pitch. As a chant progresses, the intensity increases dramatically in terms of volume, tempo, pitch range, and overall vocal fireworks. A single chant may build steadily to a climax, perhaps followed by a brief return (prior to its denouement) to the lesser level of forcefulness. More commonly, the chant may pass through several cycles of escalating intensity before its completion. The emphasis is always on facilitating total immersion into the mantra—its beauty is important here because it attracts and retains the participants' awareness and desire.

The Power of Beauty

I think that it's wise to make good use of our human weakness for beauty. If the mantras you work with are set to pleasing music, you're more likely to persevere during long stretches of repetitious chanting that might otherwise prove too tedious for you to endure. And as you'll discover, it's in abundant repetition of a mantra that it comes to be indelibly inscribed upon your mind.

Having something "stick" is a function of maximizing both your mental exposure to it and your aesthetic appreciation for it. You've undoubtedly had a melody get stuck in your head—perhaps a commercial jingle—replaying incessantly, sometimes even to the point of irritation. When working with mantras, you're exploiting this phenomenon as a positive resource. You're trying to produce a continuous mental musical "loop" while being very selective about its lyrical content. Once a mantra really gets going in your mind, it takes on a life of its own; your memory unceasingly offers its sacred content to your awareness. Music helps establish such an enduring recollection, even in the case of very long, complicated mantras.

Perhaps you've had this experience: You hear a song that you'd forgotten about for years and surprise yourself by being

35

able to sing along word for word. And while it's extremely un-likely that you would have been able to recite it without hearing the music, with the tune playing your recall is perfect and ef-fortless. As the melody unfolds, it's as if your brain is stimulated to yield its stores associated with those sounds. It's not merely lyrics, but oftentimes images, scents, and even feelings captured long before that come flooding into your awareness. Maybe you remember your grandma's house or your first crush—anything that was significant to you when that song was popular. The notes somehow awaken long-dormant impressions that were linked to your earlier musical exposure.

Similarly, the music associated with your chanting practice can be a terrific aid to your lifelong recollection of the Divine. My guru's guru, the Indian saint Neem Karoli Baba (depicted on the facing page), said, "The grace of God is being able to remember God." Being able to remember the Supreme when you need to, and thereby reliably generate an immediate ex-perience of transcendence (that which goes beyond the usual ego-bound sense of limitation) is invaluable to your happiness and well-being.

Because you'll contemplate your ideals (personified or otherwise) while doing your chanting practice, the musical dimension of the experience will become deeply fused with

Neem Karoli Baba

your meditative and worshipful activity. Then when you recall the melodies, you'll be supported in a renewed experience of absorption and devotion—even when you're not currently engaged in formal meditation or worship.

Incorporating music into your practice opens up the possibility of sharing this tool with others, fostering a profound experience of communion. There's nothing more archetypically social than singing together. The very structure of the activity —a group of people uttering the same words to the same tune (or in harmony) and tempo—lends itself to a high degree of affinity and mutual understanding. In communal chanting, participants generate and sustain a shared alignment to this or that Perfection, and thus they commonly experience a deeper sense of closeness with each other. Metaphorically speaking, it's as if several people were all approaching a single point in space; in so doing, they would necessarily come nearer to one another. The combination of voices into a single chant supports the more subtle and significant union of thoughts, feelings, values, and lives.

Having pondered the raw material of chanting—voice, mantra, and song—you're now prepared to consider the two fundamental powers of human beings, *attention* and *affection,* as they relate to the practice of devotional chanting.

Chapter Three

Attention: Chanting and the Mind

Attention and Affection: Preliminaries

The bulk of our activities are driven and organized by two primordial functions: attention and affection. These twin capacities spring from our very core, and our lives are built by exercising these powers. Beneath all the layers of attachments, aversions, masks, and cases of mistaken identity, the wisdom traditions assert that we're essentially Radiant Awareness and Care. This is the highest self of Hinduism, the awakened (*buddha*) nature of Buddhism, and the Divine nature in mystical Christianity. Consulting other belief systems, we might multiply names for this, our irreducible and indestructible essence.

Traversing a spiritual path is about growing into the basic goodness that you already fundamentally are. This reality is obscured by misguided, fickle, often self-centered operations of attention and affection. Outgrowing this defective condition requires that you extend the reach of your awareness (through attention) and care (through affection), until you completely identify with everything and everyone, no longer holding yourself separate from what you know and love.

But this growth doesn't happen overnight. As works in progress, our powers of attention and affection are more or less distracted, corrupted, and fragmented. Fortunately, they may be purified and strengthened through directing them toward things that are more worthy of your mind and heart. Until your awareness and care match that which is experienced by enlightened beings, you need to be selective about the objects of your attention and affection. This is pivotal to your progress.

42

For example, when you were a child, a favorite toy may have been the target of much of your attention and affection. As you grew up, so too did the complexity and significance of the objects that occupied your mind and captured your fancy. Today, a mere toy can't satisfy you. You require a much more meaningful target; maybe you've evolved to the point that caring for others takes the lion's share of your attention and affection.

These twin powers can mature dramatically through regular contemplation and adoration of various forms of the Supreme. Your love and concentration grow most rapidly and extensively when they're focused on an unlimited object. After such an exercise, you'll find yourself increasingly able to attend to and have compassion for more and more of the world.

If you're going to realize your potential for liberation, you need to offer your mind and heart something sweeter—more uplifting and enduring—than your usual array of regrets, reproaches, distractions, and fears. I know from experience that devotional chanting offers the very resources needed to make the best use of these indispensable human faculties. It gives your attention and affection something beyond compare to refer to in creating your precious life, moment by moment.

In this chapter, we'll examine the benefits of devotional chanting in relation to our power of attention, and in the next chapter, how the practice maximizes our capacity for affection.

Attention Defined

Attention is the selective application of awareness, a concentration of consciousness. It's your ability to direct and sustain your mental focus toward any particular object of awareness—where and how you aim your mind. There are an indefinitely large number of objects available to focus on at any given moment, but the limits of your attention span require that you narrow things down to just a few items. What you're concentrating on is an important factor in determining the quality of your present experience. This is because the objects that currently dominate your awareness are the stuff your consciousness is being organized around.

It's likely that most of your mental operations are the product of habit and happenstance, rather than conscious choice. Your mind functions according to scripts established over the course of your life, which govern what you're likely to notice, what you're prone to remember, and even how you're liable to express yourself in a given situation and the sense that you tend to make. This results in predictable, automatic responses, but it's no guarantee of their workability. Reciting mantras introduces the chance for developing greater freedom of choice in your thoughts. It offers you the opportunity to take the reins of your life so that you can steer it in a positive, purposeful direction.

44

Gaining Control Over Your Thoughts

"We live in the atmosphere of our thoughts." This is something that my guru often says. The quality of your experience in every moment—including this one—is the product of whatever you happen to be thinking at the time. Your mind is malleable, adjusting to the "shape" of whatever dominates your consciousness. While fixation on unworthy objects degrades your mind, worthy ones elevate your awareness. You can test this for yourself. Consider the following:

- How do you feel when you're thinking about something that's beautiful and inspiring to you?

- What about when you're reflecting on something that's hateful or discouraging?

What we feel clearly goes with what we're thinking about. It's important to grasp this, because we have a big problem: Our minds are distracted and defiled. We have too many objects competing for our awareness, and many of them are unworthy of our consideration. Some even corrupt our minds, polluting our thought streams with toxic images and ideas that undermine our peace, happiness, and well-being. Sometimes we aren't very discerning about our mental "diet." We take in so much information, through so many channels, but it's more than we can handle on a continuous basis without ill effects. We content ourselves with the fact that we're able to stave off boredom, but it's as if we're gorging ourselves at a buffet featuring a vast array of garbage and are pleased by the variety.

Usually we just ride the waves of whatever thoughts happen to present themselves to our consciousness, not asking where they're coming from. We don't imagine that we can select and shape our ideas or the feelings and motivations that arise with them. Nor do we recognize how profoundly we're affected, emotionally and otherwise, by the content of our minds.

But you *can* develop the ability to direct your thoughts skillfully with dedicated practice. Your mind is a creature of habit; the accumulation of your thoughts establishes a pattern that's resistant to change—a kind of "default setting" that keeps you thinking in much the same way from one moment to the next.

This is one of those good news–bad news situations. The bad news is that if your mental habits are scattered and unwholesome, without a sustained effort to reorganize them, they're likely to remain this way. The good news is that once you've undertaken such an effort, your newly focused and healthy mental habits, too, will be resistant to change, keeping you in a mental "groove" that supports your joy and welfare.

Devotional chanting supplies you with something supremely elevating to think about. Its repetitive nature is ideal for wearing new grooves in your mind, along which your thoughts may more readily travel. Over time, chanting helps you sustain a menu of beneficial thoughts that promote happiness—both in yourself and in the world you interact with. If what you're thinking correlates in some significant degree with your individual and collective quality of life, being choosy about where you direct your attention contributes to your interests and nourishes your evolution. Life is too short to spend your precious moments thinking carelessly!

Quieting Your Mind with Mantra

In the Hindu tradition, the condition of our ordinary, busy minds is likened to an insane, drunken monkey that has just been stung on the paw by a scorpion. You may not feel that this accurately describes *your* experience. However, if you try being totally silent inside for a few moments, more and more thoughts will come to mind: things to do, people to see, places to go, points that you wish you'd made in a conversation long since passed. That's a very busy monkey!

It takes a serious effort at being still to discover just how noisy you are within. Try being completely quiet inside right now for just one minute. . . . What happened? If you're like most people, your effort at silence just seemed to make your thoughts multiply. Fortunately, according to the wisdom traditions, in focusing your attention on one thing—as you do when repeating a mantra—you find peace of mind by reducing the number of voices vying for your attention. In this way, you can help yourself achieve a profound experience of inner silence.

While shifting attention all at once from the myriad voices to silence is impossible (at least for most people), "turning down the volume" to one thought at a time is feasible, even if it's challenging. When you chant, you reduce your mental chatter, what pioneering Tibetan Buddhist teacher Chögyam Trungpa called "subconscious gossip." Chanting helps you pare the overwhelming quantity of jumbled thoughts down to one—or at least a single thought at a time. You regulate your mental activity by controlling what you say to yourself. After all, what's thinking other than talking to yourself? Mantra repetition is a way of preselecting your self-talk, arranging to entertain only invocations of Perfection so that you simplify and purify your mental operations.

The goal in spiritual practice is ready access to uncluttered bliss mind, which is understood to be the permanent property of Radiant Awareness. This is ultimate silence, the unconditioned state of clarity before awareness becomes overlaid with modifications (perceptions, concepts, memories, desires, or what have you). Paradoxically, selective attention to sound is the vehicle for realizing silence. Using a single, carefully chosen sound pattern as your focus, you exclude all competing objects of awareness and settle into the pulse of the mantra. Even repeating a nonsense syllable or nonreligious word or phrase—say, *peanut butter*—will produce some measure of relief from mental chatter. It's a result of concentrating on one thing, rather than letting the mind fragment and spin off in various directions. But of course, the higher quality the thought, the greater the benefits to the thinker.

With diligent practice and the general decrease of internal noise that mantra repetition makes available, it becomes possible to simply cease all mental motion and rest (for a time at least) in the stillness that always persists in your heart-center. When the mind is still, beyond all of your usual internal noise, you're undivided, self-forgetting, and blissful.

Forgetting Yourself

Among the most interesting and important effects of chanting that I hear about and have experienced personally is the reduction of self-consciousness. This is the discomfort, awkwardness, and anxiety experienced when we're concerned about "looking good enough," when our self-esteem seems to be in jeopardy. Ironically, the remedy can't be found in further attempts to shore up our fragile egos, but rather in activities that foster an experience of self-forgetting.

Consider the situations in which you've known genuine contentment. It's likely that you were so taken up with whatever activity you were engaged in that you simply slipped your own mind as an object of your awareness. The usual cyclone of regrets, worries, to-do lists, and so forth was suspended for a period while your mind went blissfully elsewhere.

Of course, the experience of self-forgetting isn't limited to periods of spiritual practice. It happens when your mind is immersed in any sort of activity: for example, when you're totally absorbed in the unfolding narrative of an engrossing novel or film. You come back to yourself, surprised that you forgot that you were reading or viewing altogether. You were just "in" the story—and you were happy.

But these moments are generally unintentional, and they don't last. What you need is a method you can deliberately use to prolong such instances. Devotional chanting furnishes you with exactly this power. With practice, you'll be able to string together a series of self-forgetful moments. In this way, you'll generate a new orientation to everyday life, one that displaces the old bad habit of ego-clinging (what the wisdom traditions call the chronic tendency to assert yourself as a separate entity and preserve your perceived interests over those of others).

Many faith communities share the goal of reducing their members' egotism while increasing each person's identification with the Supreme or ideal Self. There are many examples of this theme being played out across traditions:

- Christ's command to "put the self to death" combined with St. Paul's admonition to "put on Christ"

- Shakyamuni Buddha's denial of the self as a permanent, independent entity, taken with the assertion that all beings are essentially awakened

- Sufism's identification of the *nafs ammara* (Arabic for "tyrannical ego") as the chief obstacle to spiritual growth

- The Hindu scriptures' oft-repeated instruction that human beings should see through our apparent separateness to our perennial condition of unity with the unborn Self of all

Devotional chanting provides a practical laboratory for exposing and examining the dualism of ordinary consciousness. This is the division of yourself from your world, subject from object; it's the chief support of your separate self-sense. Mantra practice assists you in calling your dualistic frame of mind into question and moving beyond its egocentric limitations. While repeating a mantra, you can distinguish three distinct aspects of yourself:

1. First there's the subject, which includes both you as the person chanting (the actor), and you as the observer of the chant (the witness).

2. Next comes the object, you as the one whose chanting is being observed (by the witness).

3. Finally, you may notice something that incorporates each of these aspects of yourself even as it transcends them—the Perfection addressed and made present by the mantra being chanted. It's this Perfection that you're becoming through the sincere, faithful performance of devotional chanting.

When attempting anything new and unfamiliar, it's commonplace to be self-conscious. Don't be discouraged if this happens when you first try chanting. It's normal to feel awkward, forced, perhaps even a bit clumsy, and afraid of making a mistake. I often hear participants in group-chanting events (*kirtans*) initially express reluctance to sing out loud. Sometimes they say that it's because they're uncertain how to pronounce the mantras. Often it's because they're unused to singing aloud or they're ashamed of the sound of their own voices. Many people feel squelched by memories of ridicule they've received from folks who have made fun of their singing skill, even many years before.

You may tend to be too concerned about what others might think of your performance, but I believe that you can and should beautify your chanting, for your own enjoyment as well as others'. You do so by listening to your own voice as you chant, comparing it with someone else's (live or recorded) or with the memory of how the mantra is supposed to sound. You make a change in pitch or rhythm—perhaps subtle but significant—then compare again and approve (or disapprove) of the alteration. With dedicated practice, your competence improves and your neurotic concern about how you sound is diminished.

You'll find that through your devotion to the Perfection glorified in the mantra, you become immersed in its repetition. Your dualistic orientation relaxes: The distinctions between subject and object become blurred as your identification shifts in the direction of that Perfection. As you persevere in long stretches of mantra recitation, the act of speaking or singing takes on an almost automatic quality, and your sense of being the cause of the utterance—the doer of the chanting behavior—begins to dissolve. And you'll notice that the mantra seems to take on a life of its own, chanting itself through you, almost without any sense that you're making it happen.

Through chanting, you can plunge your consciousness into ecstatic activity, a pursuit so enchanting that it takes you out of your ordinary self-involved state of mind. When you

54

repeat mantras with total focus, you forget everything else: the piles of laundry, the embarrassment your boss caused you at the last company meeting, the argument with an estranged family member that you've been replaying in your memory for years. It all dissolves. Your mind is entirely occupied with the Perfection invoked in the mantra.

This practice answers our need for a procedure that will predictably, progressively dispel our selfishness. Every time we chant, we have the opportunity to forget ourselves—even beyond the duration of the formal practice. The effects of total immersion in this devotional activity are enduring and cumulative, loosening the grip of our ego-clinging and reprogramming our mind-stream with the very sound form of the Divine.

Mantra: The Sound Form of Deity

Among the most important aspects of any mantra is the *devata*, the ideal honored and made present through it. As I explained in Chapter 1, in many cases the ideal referred to takes a personified form. I believe that this is because when human beings attempt to conceive Perfection—the ultimate good—we tend to do so in personal terms. When we envision a god or goddess, our imaginations typically run in an anthropomorphic direction: They're usually a lot like us, only more so—bigger, better, stronger, wiser, more beautiful and vivid than we perceive ourselves to be. It seems that we're unable to conceive anything more complex, more highly developed, than the human being. (Just consider the array of intelligent life-forms depicted in science fiction; they're usually humanoid.) Yet, despite our sense of human supremacy, we still locate Divinity outside of ourselves, in a being (or beings) separate from us.

56

Our efforts to approach, communicate with, and finally unite with the Supreme are typically modeled on our mundane interpersonal relationships. We tend to imagine and approach the Divine using stereotyped roles corresponding to the social functions we value most highly in our everyday lives. Since ancient times, Westerners have preferred paternal and royal images. We tend to picture God as father, king, or lord.

Not surprisingly, as the supremacy of the masculine and the monarchy has come into question, new images have emerged (or, in some cases, *re*emerged). With the rise of feminism, the Goddess has recently come to the fore. Along for the ride are other roles and associated relationships previously unavailable to Westerners as ways to interact with Deity: the Divine as child, as friend, even as lover. These represent possible ways of relating to the Supreme that are far more numerous and complex than our grandparents could have imagined.

In the early part of your spiritual practice, it's quite useful for you to picture the recipient of your devotion as existing "out there." But a more subtle understanding recognizes these deities as intelligences or excellences "in here." They're ideal cognitive forms that stand for the varied aspects of your own highest nature.

It may seem strange—perhaps even blasphemous—to say so, but the gods and goddesses who are celebrated and invoked in mantras needn't be regarded as beings existing apart from yourself; indeed, they're what is *best* in you. They're meditation deities, matchless models that metaphorically represent your ultimate aspiration in spiritual development. During episodes of contemplation, you meet them in archetypal names and forms that reflect your own highest values back to you—purity, power, wisdom, compassion—all to the *n*th degree. When you relate to them in spiritual disciplines such as devotional chanting, they inspire dedication, kindness, insight, and excellence. The deities' effect on you is no less real because they appear in your imagination—unless, of course, you treat them as unreal, foolishly diminishing them just because they don't meet you in physical bodies.

57

Just as in the *Vajrayana* tradition (the *tantric* method in Tibetan Buddhism), it's possible for you to approach your chanting practice in a way that "treats the goal as the path." This means orienting yourself to the end point of your spiritual evolution as if it were already accomplished. Look upon your idealized future as if it were your present experience. In the very act of chanting this devotional offering, you already incarnate the Perfection you're pronouncing. You summon the Divine into your body-mind continuum through increasing identification with the mantra. Repetition invites you to recognize that you're using your body-mind to presence this or that deity in sound form. This is possible because the mantras *are* the very Perfections they name and celebrate, made manifest in sound.

Hindu sages maintain that "the name of God *is* God." The Divine is made sonically, mentally, emotionally—in a word, *experientially*—present through the recitation of the name, usually in the context of a mantra. Just as an image (whether a picture or statue) represents this or that deity to you visually, a mantra represents it acoustically. What a graphic depiction of, say, Lord Shiva does for your eyes, chanting his mantra (AUM NAMAH SHIVAYA) does for your ears.

As the sound form of a given Perfection (whether personi-fied or not), each mantra is an acoustic road map to the realiza-tion of that ideal. By reciting it with devotion, you undertake the journey to that matchless destination. Using your body-mind vehicle to produce the Divine sound form, the mantra is inscribed internally, and you find yourself moving incremen-tally nearer your ultimate goal. While chanting with singleness of mind, you're *doing-being* the mantra; and once the sound form is deeply embedded in your consciousness, this upward trajectory of your attention grows and continues, even when you're silent. It's now the pattern of your becoming.

Mantras are sonic prototypes that make an array of spiri-tual insights and achievements freshly available to each new generation of chanters. By embodying the mantra's potential in devoted practice, you qualify yourself as an heir to the mer-it that's been accumulated by a long lineage of successful prac-titioners. Ideally, mantras are passed down through initiation into a spiritual relationship that commissions the recipient to preserve and extend this heritage.

If you're going to make the most of this, it would be wise to explore the possibility of receiving mantras from others who've had success with them through the grace of their own gurus (the people from whom they, in turn, received the mantras).

When you're given mantras from seasoned practitioners whose lives are saturated with their unique mental currents, you can really "hit the ground running" in your own practice. You'll have confidence that the mantras will purify your mind and heart, too, and you'll feel inspired by the promise of their potential to carry you to your teachers' favored place of freedom.

My guru, Bhagavan Das, blessing me.

When you're chanting to an ideal, you're manifesting that very Perfection in and as your own voice. Because you're always your own first audience for anything that you say or sing, at the same moment that you generate the Divine sound form with your vocal organs, you're also listening to it. The vibratory body of God or Goddess exists in and through you as you chant. You create the very sound form of the Divine with your powers of speech and present it—over and over again—to your own awareness. As you resonate with this supreme vibration, you come into increasing alignment with the ideal whose signature sound is captured in the mantra.

Your consciousness is conditioned and shaped by the things it operates on. When you meditate on your chosen ideal through the repetition of her or his mantra—especially when other competing thoughts are excluded through disciplined practice—your mind takes on the shape of your ideal. This is an internal phenomenon that's no less astonishing than if your external body were to transform into a perfect replica of this Perfection just by looking with devotion at a painting or statue depicting him or her.

The transformation of your consciousness won't happen all at once. You've developed your mental habits over a very long period of time, so it's going to take many doses of this mantra medicine to turn things around. This is a continuing process in which the rewards of having invested yourself in devotional chanting accumulate slowly. These gains affect your balance, kindness, clarity, and happiness as you come to resemble the form of the Divine you've become beneficially obsessed with through your "addiction" to its mantra.

We've seen how devotional chanting benefits our minds; now let's examine its effects upon our hearts.

Chapter Four

Affection: Chanting and the Heart

Affection Defined

Affection is the will toward union—the unquenchable impulse to be joined to, serve the interests of, and remain identified with its object. This is a more complex and refined adaptation of desire, which also involves the motivation to unite with its target but doesn't imply concern for that target's interests. The manner of attachment depends on the nature of the object. If it's something material, I might want to possess it and make it "mine," an extension of myself. If it's a favorite food, I may wish to devour it and turn it into a part of my body. If it's a person for whom I feel romantic longing, I may hope to consummate the union in the joining of our bodies. If it's some special skill, I may seek out instruction from someone who has mastered it, requesting their training and practicing it until the ability is mine.

We offer kindness and care to those we feel affection for because our kinship is so close that it dissolves at least some—and in its ultimate expression, all—sense of separation. Feeling others to be similar to ourselves, we serve their interests. The connection that we realize when we unite in affection leaves us different from what we were before. Every union involves a transcendence of our former boundaries as we take on one or more aspects of the object of affection through identification. It's no coincidence, for example, that spouses frequently come to resemble one another over the span of their lives together. Or consider the way we appropriate the mannerisms of people we admire, even when we only know of them through the entertainment media.

In brief, you become what you love. Your heart and life are organized around what you care about, and especially the people you have the highest regard for.

Reorganizing Your Attachments

There are some schools of spiritual teaching that condemn all attachments as problematic, as if every desire were equally harmful and all yearnings lead to suffering. Doubtless much of your wishing does set you up for disappointment, and even when you get what you want, you remain unsatisfied. But clearly some affections are more beneficial than others. What about the loftiest goals—say, the wish to emulate and realize the Supreme? Can these aspirations be wrong simply because they involve desire?

Devotional chanting helps you prioritize your objects of affection, encouraging you to cultivate healthy attachments to ultimately attractive and inspiring ideals—the Perfections celebrated in the words that you chant. Mantras are vehicles to generate and fervently express worshipful affinity for your highest aspiration. In and through the sound form of Perfection, you experience the bliss of devotion—you find something to lavish unparalleled care upon. Using the very breath of life and the power of voice to direct and expand your affection toward the Infinite opens your heart to the whole world. You set yourself free from the petty ego-prison that you've unwittingly built. You're no longer trapped in the narrow confines of your contracted self-concern.

Every deity that human beings have worshipped from time immemorial symbolizes one or more Perfections that we aspire to. Gods and goddesses personify such noble values as truth, power, justice, mercy, courage, wisdom, and love—affording us concrete representations of otherwise impossibly abstract notions. Mantras function as bridges to a reality beyond the senses. They engage us in direct participation in a wholeness beyond the frontier of thought, language, and imagination. While we're chanting, a goodness beyond reckoning is immediately accessible, one that from our current limited perspective may be utterly out of reach.

The process of increasingly fixing your affection upon an image of Perfection thoroughly acquaints you—and, over time, aligns you—with who you most wish to be. It's as if the mantra summons a much more evolved, future version of yourself. You're inevitably modified in the image of whatever you give your sustained care to. This is the alchemy of identification—again, you become what you love.

Identifying Your Ideals

Here's an exercise to help you clarify your ultimate values:

1. Make a list of the qualities that you most admire and would like to see in your own life. They could be courage, wisdom, generosity—anything at all.

2. Then think of someone who possesses one or more of these qualities to an extraordinary degree. It can be someone you know, a figure from history, or even a character from mythology. Identifying this personality may provide you with important clues concerning the identity of your chosen ideal—the deity that you can relate to with the fullness of your affection in order to transform your own life.

3. You may wish to do some further research to see if there's an established deity in one of the world's wisdom traditions that fits your description of your ideal (see the list of Websites and books in the Resources section at the end of this book).

My guru says, "This life is a drama that we're creating through our desires. You get what you want." It would be absurd, however, to suggest that you always receive what you casually wish for. The "getting" depends on the intensity, the single-mindedness, of the desire in question. If you want something ardently enough, you're more likely to do all in your power to obtain it. The pearl of great price in Jesus's parable could only be had at the cost of selling everything to possess it (Matthew 13:45–46).

The 19th-century Bengali saint Ramakrishna was asked if God can be seen. He affirmed that this was possible, but only "if the intensity of your longing for God is equal to the intensity of a drowning man longing for fresh air." I believe that this is true because God isn't a thing—real Deity exists in, and as, the very longing itself. When you're experiencing supreme affection, you're in the presence of the ultimate reality that people call God or Goddess. When folks approach the Divine casually, with the indifferent regard shown an uninteresting fact—something true but relatively unexciting—it's little wonder that their lives are filled with other concerns. To borrow Protestant theologian Paul Tillich's apt phrase, God is the matter of our ultimate concern.

All people have a kind of niche in their hearts reserved for the Divine. Whatever matters most to you already occupies the proper place of God in your life. This is the privileged position enjoyed by the target of your highest passion. Why not take some time to examine your own heart to discover who or what occupies that place set aside for the Supreme?

Sometimes upon reflection you may realize that your "god," the occupant of that niche, is unworthy of such an exalted post (such as when your desire is fixed upon some self-destructive addiction—gambling, for instance). Other times it's possible for you to deify that occupant. You're able to re-organize your thoughts, feelings, and actions toward that love object in a way that grants you a genuine and transformative experience of real Deity. (For example, when I worship my wife as the Divine Mother and my son as Hanuman, they evoke from me a quality of intense love that's indistinguishable from Deity.)

This emotion is an impulse that demands closeness to the beloved, and you have the opportunity to follow your attachment into transcendence. As you'll discover in greater detail in Chapter 5, you tend to take on the characteristics of people you keep company with, especially those you love intensely. Since you inevitably become what you love, you'd do well to aim high with your love. Go ahead and fix your affection on what you most wish to be, because the direction of your heart determines your future.

71

Remember when I mentioned in Chapter 3 that there are different types of relationships you can enjoy with your Divine darling? When you're relating to a given Perfection as a person, the roles that you take on imply certain ways that your affection may best be expressed. These will dictate how you approach your Divine relationship partners, not merely in chanting, but in every aspect of your life with them.

Usually the characteristics of a traditionally represented deity (sex, apparent age, personality features, and "job description," as represented in myth and iconography) suggest your role and that of your ideal—for example, child/Parent, parent/Child, servant/Master, friend/Friend, lover/Beloved. Sometimes it's possible to assume more than one role with the same deity, since it's approachable across diverse modes. For instance, you might worship the Hindu god Krishna as a mischievous toddler, as a cowherd youth, as the mighty adult chariot driver, or in his cosmic form.

This is a method that unapologetically encourages *enthusiasm* (Greek for "being filled with the Divine"). Ultimately, the distinction between you and the deity may be dispelled altogether, when you imagine yourself arising as the very Divine form that you've been worshipping. Within the bonds of your closeness, you come to know your partner so thoroughly, and your character becomes so invested with elements of theirs, that your intimacy turns into identity.

The domain of your love-wrought transformation includes, but isn't limited to, the physical dimension. Recall that in the very act of chanting the mantra of a given Perfection, you're using your body—specifically your vocal organs—to embody and realize that Perfection's sound form. However, this same process extends to the more subtle aspects of your being: your thoughts, feelings, values, and relationships. Indeed, every part of you becomes more permeated with the attributes of your Divine archetype. Each is made new by the very affection that you're offering in the act of chanting. All the wisdom traditions agree that God (by whatever name) is love. In adoring love itself, what can you become but more loving?

Singing love songs to your highest ideals helps align your heart and mind with the beloved. It's a simple yet enthralling way to boost the emotional quality of your life. By replacing unworthy targets with ultimately beautiful and inspiring ones, you're setting yourself up to fall in love with your Divine beloved over and over again. And so you're in a position to make the most of the life-shaping force of your affection.

Beauty Elevates Your Experience

Given how much you're affected by the sounds you hear—physically, emotionally, cognitively, even spiritually—arranging to offer yourself sonic splendor is simply another element in the responsible management of your life. Chanting is effective in part because it uses your ability to make and perceive sounds that are beautiful and, therefore, nourishing. Beauty is self-evidently good; like virtue, it is its own reward. By filling your life with loveliness—for all the senses, as well as for your mind and imagination—you support yourself in a more dignified condition.

Ask yourself the following questions:

- Which sounds are most pleasing to you? Could it be the crash of ocean surf, the wind rustling through leaves on a fall day, or perhaps your loved one's voice after a long absence?

- How about the noises that you find irritating or even disturbing? Maybe it's the sound of someone scraping their nails across a chalkboard, a toddler screaming in the midst of a tantrum, or the wail of a siren?

Some sounds are simply delightful, peaceful, and supportive of your well-being; others are jarring, leaving you feeling nervous and out of sorts.

The mantras you chant are set to memorable melodies marked by their simplicity and beauty. Of course, beauty is (in this case) in the ear of the beholder—what you find pleasing, someone else might regard as distasteful. So the primary musical requirement is that you choose the music that genuinely moves you, supporting the cultivation of a rich, expansive feeling-tone consistent with directly experiencing the Divine. Mantras are expressions of deep caring for your own highest ideals, so the tunes that they're sung to should sound like love songs to you. You'll probably have no trouble finding such melodies. But if you do, try singing your mantras of choice along with your favorite tunes. You'll probably be pleasantly surprised by how well this works with a bit of practice.

Just as mental immersion in mantra repetition may lead to meditative absorption and, therefore, self-forgetting, the cultivation of deeply loving feelings in and through chanting results in a kind of emotional absorption (*bhava samadhi,* a blissful state of one-pointed passion). These feelings are organized, in part, as an aesthetic response to the relative beauty of your own voice. As you discover increasing competence and grace, your absorption becomes more intense and frequent. As it does so, you also identify more deeply with the Divine subject of the mantra.

This link between the aesthetic, emotional, and relational dimensions of your devotional experience is very real and powerful. It requires that you take the matter of promoting and preserving beauty in your chanting seriously. When it comes to your practice of worship, everything is precisely as beautiful, pure, holy, and powerful as you make it. The manner of your participation has everything to do with the outcome. Your degree of emotional investment is tied to the intensity of your adoration. Just as the amount of thought you put into choosing a gift for someone may suggest the level of your regard, the splendor of your effort in worship determines the likely value of your experience. You owe it to yourself and the world you share your being with to beautify your life in this way as best you can.

Investment Leads to Identification

When you make an offering of your own voice in chanting, you infuse your imagination with Divine energy, and your devotion increases through investing your precious resources of time and love in what's most meaningful to you. In every act of devotion there's an element of sacrifice—if only of the modest sort implied by the fact that you could be doing something else with your valuable time.

Very early in our relationship, my guru told me to get up every morning at 3 A.M. and chant nothing but "RAM" for two and a half hours over a period of 30 days. At the time, I was a college professor with a heavy teaching load, so this represented a considerable inconvenience, to say the least. But I did it, and by persevering in the practice, I learned firsthand how commitment goes with investment. It brought home the lesson that an offering of love is its own reward. Devotional chanting provides opportunities to make regular, disciplined gifts of our very selves to that which inspires us.

I encourage you to make—and keep—a commitment to yourself to set aside some time every day for devotional service to your ideal. And it should be enough time that you feel that it represents a meaningful expenditure of this most precious resource. Jesus said that "where your treasure is, there will your heart be also" (Luke 12:34). Your affections run toward those things and people in which you've made a substantial investment.

It was only after I went through the discomforts associated with the constant care and feeding of my then-infant eldest son, Tristan, that I first realized the truth of this. I came to increasingly love him and identify with him as a direct result of the inconvenience I suffered on his behalf. As I poured more of myself into his care, I found myself caring more *for* him.

So it is with any devotional practice you take on. Presenting your steadfast efforts as a living sacrifice to your ideal establishes and sustains an evident bond between you and the Divine. What begins as a dutiful and, perhaps, obligatory offering to a (seemingly) external ideal develops into a spontaneous celebration of your own inherent Divinity. When you chant, you can surrender your life so totally to your supreme values that any lingering sense of separateness gradually disappears.

Moving from "Out There" to "In Here"

As beings who have grown up knowing only the relative truth of attachment and aggression between divided individuals, we must start where we are. Our openness to and identification with the Supreme is limited by the fact that our affection is expressed within boundaries established in our minds. We're trained to accept without question the illusory separateness of ourselves from our ideals, from other people, and from everything outside our own bodies.

This is why it's useful to begin with the worship of a form. As long as you continue to identify exclusively with your physical self and fail to recognize the utter interdependence— even the unity—of all apparently separate beings, you must make certain concessions to your dualistic thinking. That means choosing a form of the Divine that attracts you and offering your time, energy, gifts—and ultimately yourself—in devotional activity such as chanting.

Love must have an object, something you may aim your affection toward and identify with. It's impossible for you to care for nothing. A Divine form provides an excellent target for your devotion—and mantras are like arrows that you let fly, allowing you to plunge straight into this supreme objective. As this practice becomes more central to your life and your feelings are ripe with the remembrance of Deity, you'll shed your obsessive self-concern. As you invest yourself more and more fully in the deity "out there," you'll gradually develop the very excellences and attributes of the deity "in here" as stable features of your own character.

A committed chanting regimen invites you to adopt multiple perspectives: You'll perceive yourself first as singer, then as audience, and finally (with dedicated practice) as song. This is similar to the shifts in perspective you may experience by participating in chanting's cousin, ritual worship. You can find yourself imaginatively occupying several roles—the one making the offering, the offering itself, and ultimately, the deity receiving the offering. Such a process is a potent form of mind training that multiplies your points of view. It loosens the grip of "single vision," the narrow-minded, selfish mentality that so often ensnares you. It permits you to experience the world in a manner that's less confined by the egoic, "I'm the center of the universe" perspective that dominates your ordinary consciousness and fuels your suffering.

Emotional Yoga

This path of affection is a yoga of emotion. It's anchored in the venerable *bhakti yoga* tradition, the method of "union through devotion." Like its counterpart emphasizing physical training—hatha yoga—devotional chanting involves adopting certain preselected "postures." Metaphorically speaking, you can use beneficial attitudes and emotions to "stretch" yourself by undertaking challenging exercises that bring you to, and beyond, the horizon of your abilities (that is, feeling more intensely and with greater selectivity and purpose than you previously thought possible). You can improve your "flexibility" and range of extension (namely, become less reactive, more adaptive, and more capable of identifying with a greater portion of the world) and integrate fragmented aspects of yourself (in other words, learn to love your highest ideals, yourself, and even unpleasant others).

Your Devotional Practice

Devotional chanting is best approached as a vital component in a sustained, comprehensive program. It should be a discipline that addresses and supports your health, happiness, peak performance, and evolution across the several dimensions of your being.

Take a moment to review the way you care for yourself. Can you identify some concrete, positive activity that you routinely perform in service of your well-being across every facet of your life? If not, select one thing that you can add to your daily schedule in each of the following five areas:

1. Physical
2. Intellectual
3. Emotional
4. Relational (Interpersonal)
5. Spiritual

Because every aspect of your life is interconnected with all the others, such an integrated approach to your well-being is most effective.

Your Chanting Environment

As you'll see in Chapter 5, it's important to take part in devotional chanting as a communal activity (just as people undertake a portion of their hatha yoga training in the social atmosphere of classes and workshops) and enjoy the stimulation shared in intensive group worship. However, it's also crucial for your growth in this yoga of emotion that you create a foundation of private, solitary practice.

I believe that you absolutely must establish a regular routine of formal ritual worship, with devotional chanting at its heart. If you've grown up with the notion that religious observances should be limited to a church or temple, it may at first seem a bit odd to set aside time every day to lavish affection on your chosen ideal. Devotional chanting, together with prayer (conversation with the Supreme) and offerings (gifts given to and received from your deity), may be performed anywhere, anytime. But having a special place and time set aside exclusively for this yoga of emotion helps maintain your spiritual routine and bolsters the effects of your practice. Fill this place and time with everything most lovely to you: statues and pictures of your ideals, teachers, and other loved ones. Adorn your shrine with incense, fresh flowers, candles, and other auspicious and inspiring ornaments.

My own shrine is populated with statues and paintings of the meditation deities that I'm most attracted to. Those from the Tibetan Buddhist *Vajrayana* tradition are the most numerous and include the female Buddha, Vajravarahi; the cosmic Buddha couple, Samantabhadra and consort, in *yab-yum* (the seated posture of union); Avalokiteshvara, *bodhisattva* (awakened being) of compassion; and Vajrasattva, the primordial Buddha of indestructible reality, right next to his peaceful manifestation, Akshobya. Green Tara and Vajrakilaya, the fierce dharma protector, are there, too.

From the Hindu tradition, there's Lord Shiva, Kali Ma, Ganesha, Hanuman, and Durga. I also include photos of my guru, significant figures in our lineage, and my wife and sons. Lastly, there's an array of implements I use in formal ritualistic worship, including a bell, prayer wheel, *dorje* (stylized thunderbolt scepter), *phurba* (ritual dagger), and *damaru* (small two-headed drum).

This is where I sit with the Supreme, so it's a place that's so charming, so consecrated to worship, that when I enter it, I find myself immediately caught up in its enchantment and can easily carry on with my devotion.

When you chant in such an environment, you're able to directly address the visual forms of the very Perfections you're invoking in sound. Combined with other traditional offerings (water, sweets, fresh flowers, incense, and lamplight), the presentation of your own voice in this sacred atmosphere generates an engaging sensory experience that supports deep feeling. This is a place you'll return to again and again, sanctifying it through devotion with each visit.

By putting yourself through the paces of this emotional yoga, you'll give yourself the chance to love more deeply and expansively than you have before. Here you may exercise your

Kurt A. Bruder

capacity for compassion in regular "workouts" of focused ado-ration. It's a training regimen for your affection, and the long-term results of this routine will yield a more concentrated and encompassing love than you've ever been capable of. As the 19th-century Russian mystic Madame Swetchine famously ob-served, "To love deeply in one direction makes us more lov-ing in all others." You're in this for the highest conceivable purpose: to maximize the love you're able to experience and share. Why would you do this halfway?

Having taken stock of the ways that devotional chanting operates inside of us, in the next chapter let's consider how this practice may be shared with others.

རྫོགས་པ་ཆེན་པོ་ཀློང་ཆེན་སྙིང་ཐིག་གི་སྔོན་འགྲོའི་ངག་འདོན། དྲི་མེད་ཞིང་དུ་བགྲོད་པའི་ཐེམ་སྐས། ཀུན་ཐོབ་བླ་ན་མེད་པའི་ས་བོན་འདེབས།

བདམས་པ་བདམས། ཁ་ཆེམས་ནས་བདག་ལ་དགྱེས་པ་སྩོལ། ཨོ་ཡ་སྐྱབ་ག་ནུ་ག་ར་ཙ་སབ་ར་སྣྱ་ར་ལྔུ་ར་ཨེ་ནི་པ་ཏི་ནི་ཧྱ་ལེ་སྒྲུབ། ཚེ་ཚོས་ལ་སྒྱུ་འཕྲུལ་དྲ།

སྦྱི་ ཀུ་ཡི་ ཤུ་ཡ་ལ་ ག་ནི་ ནི་ཙིད། གླུ་ཏ་འཕྲུལ་གྱི་ཟ་སྐྱོང་ སྣ། ཀ་གཅལ་ནས་སགོ་ཚོགོ་ཚོ་ཚི་དུ་ཏུ་ར་ནི་ཧ། དགའ་བོ་ཞི་སག་ཚོ་གི་སྐྱིད་ཕྱུག

ཆོས། ཁྱུད་ལ་དར་བདུའ་བའི་ནོ་དོན་མཛད། ཧ་ཇི་འཛིན་གྱི་ཉ་སྒྲུབ་ལ་ཐུགག་འཚོ་བོ། ཀྱུ་ན་ནི་ཧ་ཇི་ར་རྒྱལ་བའི་ཟོགག་ཏུ་ཉེ་ར་བཙུབམས་བ། ཉིའ།

ཞི་འདི་ནག་གི་རྒྱལ་བཙོ་བཟུམ། ཉི་ས་སུ་གདུད་ད་ག་བག་ར་སྒྱུ་ཉ་ཆེན་གྱིས། ཧ་ར་ནད་ཙུ་ར་ས་ཅོག་ན་གུ་ཞ་ན་གུ་བ་ན་ཉི། ཆེ

པའི་འབྱུང་པོ་དཔལ་བ་སེ་བ། ཁ་ན་པ་ཆེ་ཆེ་རྒྱུན་དུ་བ་ན་ན་ཧ། ཀ་ཚོ་བི་ཧེ་ན་ཁལས་སུ་ཧ་ར་ཧ་ར་དུབས་འ

ཆུ་ག་ཏུ་རྒྱུ་ལ་པ་ར་ས་ཚོང་། ཚེ་ཉི་ཧུ་ན་ཟོ་ག་ཅ་ཙི་དང་བྱ་ར། ཡ་སྐྱུ་ག་ཆ་ད་ར་པ་བི་ཏི། དྲི་ཟི་ལེ་སྣ་དི། ཤུ་ཏི་ཧི་སེ་སྒྲུབ། ཚི་ཧི་ཡི་སྒྲུ་ཚུ། དུ་ད་ད་ར་ཟེཿ ཧ་ཧ་ཧ། ཁ་ད་ཡ་ད་ནུན་ཁ་ཅ་རས་ཧ་བ་ས་ལ། ཧ་ར་སུ་ག་ན་ད་ཧེ་བ་སགྱ་ར། ཆེ་སུ་གདུན་རྒྱལ་ཞ་ཉི་སྒྱ། ཨེ་ཧྱི་ལི་སྒྱི་སྒྱིཿ

Chapter Five

Chanting
Together

Solitary and Communal Practice

Unless you have the good fortune to live in a monastery or ashram where devotional chanting is a regular part of an everyday group practice, it's likely that you'll be doing the bulk of it alone. As I mentioned in the last chapter, solitary worship is an essential element in your comprehensive spiritual training. This is because it establishes your sincerity by undercutting the egocentric impulse to parade your spiritual activities and achievements before the eyes of others.

Jesus spoke directly to this issue: "But whenever you pray, go into your room and shut the door and pray to your Father who is in secret; and your Father who sees in secret will reward you" (Matthew 6:6). This isn't to suggest that you must avoid spiritual practice in the presence of others; indeed, both solitary and communal worship are imperative to your progress. I advocate regular group chanting, but I still feel that you should make sure that "being seen" isn't the motive for your participation, since such narcissism negates devotion.

There are opportunities for accelerating your evolution that are uniquely available through interpersonal relationship and collaborative activity. You're likely to get more out of communal chanting if you understand certain things about the social dimension of your life.

Playing at the Boundary Between the One and the Many

It's a commonplace idea that individuals compose a community, but it's equally, if less obviously, the case that the community creates the individual. The world's wisdom traditions have long recognized how important our associations are in fashioning our identities. For example, among the most valued and regularly mentioned concepts in Buddhism are the Three Jewels—*Buddha* (the awakened ideal), *Dharma* (the method for awakening), and *Sangha* (the community of those who are trying to wake up together). These are also known as the three objects of refuge, because Buddhists understand that each is a shelter from the hazards of cyclical existence. Without the ideal, the method, and the community, individuals are likely to remain asleep, ignorant of their true condition as Radiant Awareness and Care. Together members maintain a safe, stimulating environment for collaborative procedures for awakening.

Making the most of your opportunities for enlightenment means recognizing your interdependence with others and fortifying yourself by participating in communal spiritual practice. But your ability to derive benefit from your association with others—even if it's just a group of people you occasionally chant with—may be limited by your persistent belief in the permanence of your own independent existence.

Individuality is highly valued in our society, at least up to the point where our actions and attitudes threaten our membership within the larger community. We're supposed to "fit in," even when we "stand out." We've been trained all our lives to assume that we're unique and disconnected from every other person. But this self-conception has its origin in assumptions that tend to blind us to a deeper and more accurate perception of reality.

You've always existed in a condition of profound interdependence with beings apparently outside of you. You're already connected to everyone and everything, but your tendency is to think of yourself as an isolated entity. Some of your associations are obviously central to your life, such as those with your parents and other influential people. Others seem to have relatively little impact on you—it's difficult to recognize the effect of someone living in another part of the world or in a different period in history. Yet even in those cases where the relationship between you and others is obvious, your sense of independence persists. You insist upon your separateness despite the clearest evidence of connection across all dimensions of your experience, whether physical, biological, emotional, intellectual, or spiritual.

Take the case of your seemingly separate body. Your skin appears to form a boundary marking the division between you and the rest of the universe, yet your physical life depends on an ongoing exchange of matter and energy across this barrier. Oxygen comes in, carbon dioxide goes out; food comes in, waste goes out. What was "not you" becomes "you" for a time; when it leaves the body, you view it as "not you" again.

92

More subtle—and profound—interactions permit you to maintain life in other domains of experience: feelings, ideas, commitments, goals, and so on. These are routinely exchanged in the give-and-take of everyday life with apparently separate others. If this very idea, for example, finds a place in your thinking, then something that was seemingly outside of you is now inside you as a part of your mind. And if it should find its way into your speech or otherwise affect your actions, it's rippling out from you into a world of so-called independent individuals.

Given the fact that every aspect of your life has this interdependent quality, it would be naïve and stubborn to cling to the notion of radical separateness from others. The boundaries that you'd supposed were so fixed and certain turn out to be blurred and permeable. Currents of energy and information transcend every conceivable border in a vast network of dynamic relatedness. So where does one individual stop and another begin?

We've all internalized thoughts, feelings, attitudes, beliefs, mannerisms, figures of speech, values—a host of subtle elements of our shared humanity—from an incalculably vast array of sources. An honest examination of the relationships that have shaped your interests, opinions, and values (for starters) will immediately reveal just how much of "you" comes from someone else. Put simply, "out there" is already "in here" (and vice versa). Where's the boundary now?

The Group Dynamic as a Resource for Transcendence

Genuinely appreciating the mutually dependent nature of our lives and of all things requires that we question the mistaken notion that each of us is an independent entity. This insight into the true nature of reality is called *śūnyatā,* commonly translated as "emptiness," and is among the central philosophical tenets of Buddhism. This isn't emptiness in the ordinary sense, but is a term used to describe that fact that there isn't a single phenomenon in the entire universe that's self-caused. Nothing possesses inherent existence or intrinsic reality; rather, each thing and event is the result of a far-reaching network of interdependent causes and conditions. This is emphatically true of our personalities, too: None of us caused ourselves to be. We're "works in progress," being fashioned even now by a vast array of influences—some that we're scarcely even aware of.

Perhaps a visual metaphor might be useful to illustrate *śūnyatā.* Every person we encounter, and especially those we share our community with, is like a mirror, reflecting some version of ourselves in their moment-by-moment response to us; and we provide the same reflection for each of them. We're all mirrors reflecting other mirrors.

Have you ever been in a hallway or an elevator with two parallel mirrors on either side of you? Maybe you recall the extraordinary spectacle of a vast number of repeating, reflected images, each slightly smaller than the next. But these images don't go on forever; rather, they seem to curve off to one side. Why can't you see all the way to infinity? Well, put simply, you're in your own way. If it weren't for the obstruction created by your own head (here representing ego-clinging), you could see forever.

When you remain ignorant of the radical truth of emptiness, your compulsive self-grasping limits your vision, awareness, and care. But once you begin to experience the world—and yourself—in terms of emptiness, you're free to see, know, and love in new ways. You can cease taking yourself quite so seriously and lighten up a bit.

I'd like to suggest three important ways for you to make use of this insight:

1. Examine your personal life so that you comprehend to what extent you're shaped by your interpersonal attachments. Getting in touch with the range and depth of influences you've accrued by sharing life with other specific people vividly brings home the truth of emptiness. From a

conventional perspective, to a considerable degree, you are who you're with.

2. Expand your sympathies and your resources for facing life's challenges by increasing the number, variety, and depth of your connections with the deities invoked and glorified in the mantras you chant. The Perfections you worship are the ultimate community that you identify with, and keeping company with your ideals in devotional practice will elevate you. In their presence you're at your best; the effects of your regular interaction with them accumulate over time and show up in your character and abilities.

3. Although you can't do anything to alter the constellation of connections that have shaped your life until now, you do enjoy considerable freedom to choose your future associations. Knowing that you're linked with all others, you can selectively cultivate attachments and activities with those who are most likely to be uplifting, inspiring, and supportive of mutual development. If you truly are who you're with, choosing the people you're with and how you're with them means deciding who you'll be.

Kirtan: Collaborative Chanting

Given our interdependent nature as human beings, group devotional chanting, or *kirtan* (from the Sanskrit *kirt,* meaning "to praise"), is an exceptionally beneficial activity that's ideally suited to our need for an enjoyable, user-friendly, efficient, and helpful practice. It also brings together a cross section of practitioners spanning diverse personal histories and levels of spiritual maturity.

Devotional chanting is essentially interactive. It's an exemplary social experience—even when you're practicing alone. The very structure of chanting reveals a dynamic, communal quality. You can see this in everything from its call-and-response organization (the leader sings a line, then the other participants repeat it in the same tune) to the multiple roles and perspectives that you're invited to take while chanting. In addition, it always involves you in dialogue with some representation of the Supreme. This is the Divine other who is addressed and invoked and with whom you seek to connect—and ultimately merge—through devotional chanting.

Communal chanting comes before solitary practice, just as dialogue comes before monologue. This is a matter both of preeminence and timing. The prototypical experience of chanting

97

takes place in the company of like-minded others. Just as children acquire language largely by being included in conversation with their parents, participants gain proficiency by blending their voices, minds, and hearts with other practitioners. The less experienced follow the lead of more seasoned veterans.

Devotional chanting is an idealized form of communication. In addition to refining attention and expanding affection, it satisfies significant social needs. As you now know, this activity provides a means to realize union with the Divine, but it's also a procedure for developing solidarity with others. Indeed, this practice is at its pinnacle when it's shared, when we chant as a community. Even in nonreligious group settings—for example, at sporting events, during labor-union strikes, among picketing protesters, or at a political rally—you're likely to find a great number of people building connection with one another by chanting the same phrase or slogan.

When we intone mantras together, all of the benefits that are available in solitary chanting are magnified, sometimes to such a degree that the results suggest a different order of practice altogether. In group chanting we're able to take advantage of the well-recognized social phenomenon of positive synergy. Uniting the energies of multiple participants results in an outcome much greater than what can be accounted for by tallying the individuals' distinct contributions. The commonality of purpose yields an exponentially greater experience than is typical for the solitary chanter. Because the group is functioning as a coherent living system, "the whole is greater than the sum of its parts." The amplification of the effects of devotional chanting in the energized atmosphere of kirtan is unmistakable. It's something you can feel in every aspect of your being.

Group chanting also introduces certain unique possibilities:

— The prospect of aesthetic excellence, creativity, and complexity is greatly enhanced with the multiplication of voices and instruments. As we move from soloist to symphony, the range of sonic intensity and harmonic intricacy is dramatically increased. The result: a heightened encounter with beauty.

— There's also an energy that's palpably present in the mix of many voices. While difficult to define, it's nevertheless conspicuously absent in solitary chanting. In the fusion of our devotion-inspired voices, we feel the vibration that we're creating together—not just in our ears, but in the very core of our being. This is quintessential communion: nourishing others with the fruit of our devotional activity and in return receiving more than we could ever hope to give away.

— In the context of group chanting, participants some-times experience a relaxation of the conventional boundaries between their (apparently) separate selves, leading to previ-ously uncharacteristic levels of openness, vulnerability, gener-osity, and compassion. You'll notice that the soothing, consol-ing, and encouraging effects of group chanting soften your ordinary ego defenses. Don't be surprised when this results in a less "brittle," reactive disposition. These outcomes must, of course, be sustained and extended in your sadhana—but you'll no doubt observe noticeable gains after just one kirtan.

— Some surprisingly powerful group processes may account for the benefits of kirtan. Such predictable, well-documented structures of social influence as peer pressure, reduced inhibi-tions, and "group-think"—mechanisms that operate in any col-lective—are especially evident among members who have con-siderable history with one another and the practice of chanting. Communal devotional chanting exploits these features of the group dynamic for commendable spiritual ends: the well-being, happiness, and evolution of all involved.

— Finally, communal chanting will likely bolster your per-sonal devotional practice and related methods for awakening.

When you feel the results of entering and contributing to the unique energetic field of inspiration, grace, and empowerment of a kirtan, you may discover the motivation you need to persevere in a thoroughgoing spiritual discipline. Doing so strengthens your whole community, since the benefits you generate in private sadhana tend to overflow when you chant in the company of others.

Finding a Chanting Group

You may want to start chanting with others but be at a loss about how to locate such a group. Since this practice has proliferated in the wake of hatha yoga, it's a good idea to contact local yoga studios to inquire if they know of any kirtans being offered in the area. Alternative-healing centers and metaphysical bookstores are also potential venues for chanting events, and they can be great sources of information.

There are a growing number of resources available online, too. Chant-related Web-based bulletin boards, blogs, forums, and so forth can help you learn about who's chanting where and when. The key is to connect with others who are interested in this activity. Once you meet some fellow chanters, you should have little difficulty finding out about what's available in your region. You can also use your favorite search engine to scout for events—type in the words *kirtan, chant,* and the name of your location to get started.

It may be that there's already an established gathering of chanters who meet regularly nearby. Some groups have a local, "in-house" kirtan wallah (leader); others are facilitated by more than one person. Many times a loose community of chanters will show up at events led by one or more visiting wallahs who periodically present in the area.

Features of a good chanting group include:

- A warm, welcoming attitude toward newcomers

- An openhearted perspective regarding varieties of spiritual belief and practice

- Freedom from sectarianism

- Capable (although by no means "professional") musical leadership without "look at me" showmanship

- A general atmosphere of devotion (the most important characteristic)

If you're unable to find an adequate group in your area, give serious thought to organizing one yourself. Many chanting veterans got their start participating in kirtans that they hosted in their homes (or those of interested friends), simply sharing the fruit of their private practice as best they could. My own first efforts at leading kirtan were in such situations, with several of the folks present taking a turn before passing the opportunity on to the next fledgling leader.

It might also be helpful if you sponsored a visit by an experienced kirtan wallah. Securing the help of someone who is able to provide instruction and inspiration in chanting can really set a novice group in motion. I myself love lending a hand in this way (and would welcome the opportunity, if you'd care to contact me), and I know other kirtan wallahs do, too.

Now let's shift our attention to the mantras themselves. In the next chapter, I've assembled 14 potent sound forms of Perfection for you to bring into play. These are valuable resources that you can draw upon over a lifetime of devotional chanting.

Chapter Six

Vocalizing the Sound Form of the Divine

From Theory to Practice

Up to this point, you've been learning about devotional chanting in terms of its origins and components, how it affects your mind and heart, and its communal expression. Now it's time to acquaint yourself with a collection of mantras you can use to apply all that you've learned. You're ready to experience the benefits of devotional chanting firsthand.

In the following pages, I offer some background information on each of the mantras included on the accompanying CD. The selections are motivated by my wish to provide you with an assortment that will support general spiritual development, as well as addressing a variety of specific needs. My explanations of the mantras are based in part on my having chanted them a good deal—often in connection with other related practices, such as visualizing the Perfections celebrated in each one. At several points, I offer allegorical interpretations of myths and legends associated with the deities and other figures that most of the mantras memorialize. I believe that you can gain a lot of valuable insight by approaching the figures and exploits in these venerable stories as symbols that reveal important lessons about the human condition.

I don't claim to exhaust the meaning of the mantras presented here; rather, I merely suggest some ideas that have fortified my own understanding and devotion. Indeed, I expect that you'll discover much more about their significance and value as you explore them on your own.

The recordings are presented as models for your own practice. Please sing along, just as if we were in the same room chanting together. Vocal skill is a product of careful listening coupled with profuse repetition. I'd encourage you to sit upright (whether on a cushion or in a chair), with a straight back—this will help you breathe easily as you chant. You might choose to work with a particular mantra on the CD for a time, setting your player to repeat that track over and over as you sing along. When you're able to chant with the recording, try doing so on your own. Once you feel comfortable with this, you can move on to another mantra.

This is a learning process involving the imitation of a standard. You're invited to produce the same dynamic sequence of sounds that you're hearing, using your own voice as your instrument. With practice, you'll sound more and more like what you listen to on the CD. Eventually, you'll be chanting these mantras on your own and perhaps creating new tunes to go with them and others.

At first you may find yourself stuck, unable to chant aloud without embarrassment, even with no one else around . . . but please don't give up. Remember how you used to sing constantly when you were young? From the time you were a little baby, you played with your voice—and it was great fun. It's likely that somewhere along the line another person said something that made you feel self-conscious about your ability, and that put an end to your joy in singing. It may take a while to get comfortable, but you'll find yourself more relaxed and self-confident with a bit of perseverance.

Once you've had some practice in private, find an outlet where you can chant in a crowd—where you won't be singled out. Ideally, this will be in kirtans, but you can get this kind of experience anywhere people gather to sing. By this time, chances are that you'll sound a lot better than when you first started. After practicing along with favorite recordings and in the company of other people, you'll develop an ear for matching the sounds you're aiming for with your voice.

The mantras on the CD obviously vary in text and tune—but they also differ in relative complexity, meaning, and the specific effects that they're used to generate. All of them will be helpful in calming and concentrating your mind, elevating your feelings, expanding your compassion, and realizing your own awakened nature. But as you acquaint yourself with them, the Perfections they invoke, and their effects on your body-mind continuum, you'll distinguish particular applications for each. Like a craftsman who has a variety of tools at his disposal, each suited to a particular task, you now have the array of sound forms needed to build a life that you love. On one occasion you may require physical healing; on another your pressing need might be courage. Visualize the Perfection that you're presencing through the mantra (whether personified or not), and have faith that you're coming into alignment with it.

Remember that a mantra is a path to the Perfection that it invokes. Each repetition takes you a step closer to stable residence in that very ideal.

Vital Mantras

1. The All-Inclusive Mantra

AUM

AUM is the primordial mantra. It's the first cosmic sound out of which all other vibrations were born and into which they all dissolve. Although often written as "OM," this syllable is composed of three letters (and their corresponding distinct sounds)—*A, U,* and *M:*

- *A* is the sound of basic vocalization, unaltered by the organs of speech beyond the vocal cords.

- *U* builds on that basic vocalization, shaping it with the open mouth.

- *M* involves the last site where vocal sound can be modified—the lips, which are closed, requiring that the utterance be expressed through the nasal passage, as when humming.

Because each of its three letters is associated with a different site of sound production, moving from the beginning (vocal cords) to the end (lips) of our vocal machinery, AUM encompasses the full range of sounds that human beings can produce. It's understood to be the sum and substance of all words that can be spoken—and so is revered for containing all mantras within itself.

Many interpretations have been offered for the significance of this trinity of letters. Most emphasize the way AUM is used to convey the sense of all-inclusive totality. It's been associated with many other historic "threes" of spiritual interest, including:

- The three times—past, present, and future

- The three principal Hindu deities and their respective spheres of responsibility—Brahma (creation), Vishnu (preservation), and Shiva (destruction)

- The three *gunas* (Sanskrit for "qualities of nature")—*sattva* (essence, harmony); *rajas* (activity, passion); and *tamas* (inertia, sloth)

Among the most interesting connections is that to the three states of consciousness: waking, dreaming, and deep dreamless sleep. The vast silence in which these three letters occur is called *turya* ("the fourth")—consciousness itself.

Although AUM is a common element included in many mantras, it may be chanted by itself to great benefit, as it produces a terrific restorative effect on your awareness—a bit like rebooting a computer's hard drive. I recommend chanting AUM in a slow, drawn-out manner, allowing the sound of each of the three letters to arise, abide for a time, and then transition into the next. Rest in the silence for a while before intoning the mantra again. Remember that you're making and hearing the sound from which all worlds and beings spring into existence, so AUM should be approached with the greatest reverence.

2. Beginning Well *(Ganesha)*

AUM GANG GANAPATAYE NAMAHA SWAHA
GANG GANAPATAYE NAMO NAMAH
GANESHA SHARANAM JAI JAI GANESHA
AUM. I bow to Ganesha (Lord of Categories). So be it!
GANG [Ganesha's signature sound].
I bow to Ganesha again and again.
I take refuge in Ganesha. Hooray, hooray for Ganesha!

Ganesha is one of the most universally loved deities in India. With his elephant head and chubby little-boy body, he's a comical figure, jovial and mischievous. Ganesha is the lord of thresholds, the transitional spaces between things. He's also the god of beginnings and is associated with the earth, the foundation upon which all things rest. As the lord of Muladhara, the root *chakra* (energy center) at the base of the spine, Ganesha cares for your basic survival and safety needs.

His presence is invoked whenever folks who are inspired by him begin something new—especially when the endeavor is important. Remembering the Divine as you begin something is a way of committing yourself to achieving the best that you can imagine in that venture. As my guru says, "How it begins is how it ends."

Ganesha

Ganesha is also known as the remover of obstacles. Suppose that you had to get somewhere urgently in the middle of a blizzard and suddenly found yourself driving behind a snowplow that cleared your way right to your destination . . . that's Ganesha at work. Obviously, you face obstacles in the external world, but the most troublesome ones you encounter are those aspects of yourself where you remain ignorant, selfish, and undeveloped. The blockages that pop up in your life are tailor-made to expose those areas where you're stuck. Your obstacles are most likely different from mine or anybody else's. Each calls for a higher level of performance than you were capable of prior to meeting it.

Elephants are big and difficult to move if they choose to stay put. Ganesha is the remover of obstacles, but he can be usefully recognized *as* each obstacle, too. The usual response to an impediment is to resent and curse it. But what if you shifted your perspective and could see the Divine winking at you through the blockage, playfully goading you to rise up and overcome it with gratitude and renewed effort? Maybe the hurdle could be more easily surmounted if you saw it as a gift that encourages you to grow? Worshipping Ganesha provides an opportunity to rethink your obstacles in this way.

Many Hindu deities are depicted as having *vahana* (Sanskrit for "vehicles"): Shiva has his bull, Nandi; Durga has her lion, Mrigaraj; Vishnu has his eagle, Garuda. Ironically, Ganesha's vehicle is a little mouse, Mushika. Isn't that just perfect? After all, what better creature to move an elephant?

The mouse, or rat represents your petty ego, on which Ganesha rides. When you forget yourself in chanting to him, he moves in response to your "squeaking." In your worshipful submission to your obstacle *du jour,* you're overturning your ordinary reaction of resistance and complaint. Instead, you invite Ganesha to saddle you in this form until you genuinely rise to the occasion, growing in those ways that could only be achieved in response to this very challenge.

Once that work is accomplished, there will be a new obstacle as surely as there will be a fresh beginning, and with it will come another opportunity to develop in yet another dimension of your life. But maybe with practice you can learn to remember that the Divine is hiding in your challenges. Then perhaps you can bear their weight with gratitude and grace in the certainty that they'll strengthen you if only you can learn to welcome them.

3. Changing Your Trajectory *(Saman Mantra)*

**ASATO MA SAT GAMAYA
TAMASO MA JYOTIR GAMAYA
MRITYOR MA AMRITAM GAMAYA
AUM SHANTI SHANTI SHANTIHI**
*Lead us from the unreal to the Real,
From darkness to Light,
From death to Immortality.
AUM. Peace, peace, peace be upon us all.*

This mantra—from the ancient Hindu scripture, the *Brihad-Aranyaka Upanishad*—is a series of requests directed toward your own awakened essence that you should progress from your temporarily distorted condition of illusion, ignorance, and self-destruction to your actual being as essential, radiant, and living awareness. Sometimes your thoughts and actions may be so neurotic and distracted that you're unable to access the peace that's perpetually available within your heart-center. Taking the time to get in touch with that abiding stillness is crucial to your well-being and to the unfolding of your deep potential.

In this mantra, you'll find an example of a sound form for a Perfection that isn't personified—no representation of a deity is involved here. Rather, by repeating these syllables, you express a complex wish to change the direction of your life. It's a request for a threefold shift from your habitual self-centered, yet ironically self-sabotaging, way of life to a new and authentic approach.

We commonly relate to fleeting, constantly changing illusions—such as our own separate selves—as if they were real, permanent, independently existing entities. Conversely, our tendency is to regard the most real—preeminently, our essential nature as luminous awareness—as an inaccessible dream. Similarly, many times we disregard genuine knowledge (direct experience of what is the case, prior to all categories of thought and beyond all means of expression), preferring the pale substitute of labels and ready-made theories. Finally, we seek to nourish our bodies, minds, and spirits on poisons (especially ignorance, clinging, and hatred), doing all that we can to defend and expand ego, while snubbing those things that enliven and elevate us.

Rather than remaining in this topsy-turvy condition, you appeal to your own innate clarity for its blessed reversal through this mantra. Of course, while wishing to be reoriented in this way is an important first step, you must persevere in your intention to remain in reality, light, and immortality. This requires that you choose this new direction over and over again. Reciting this mantra is a way of deeply ingraining this intention in your body-mind vehicle.

4. Invoking the Formless Supreme *(Shiva)*

AUM NAMAH SHIVAYA
AUM. I bow down to Shiva (the Auspicious One).

Lord Shiva is the third of three foremost deities in Hinduism: Brahma, the creative principle; Vishnu, the preserving principle; and Shiva, the destroying principle. "God of destruction" is a pretty scary job description. While it seems like a bad thing, taking a more ecological perspective allows you to acknowledge the inescapability of change and impermanence. Nothing that exists is simply unmade; instead, everything is transformed over time into other things. This perpetual recycling is a necessary feature of the universe; without it, things

Shiva

Kurt A. Bruder

would be frozen in a static condition, devoid of life or the possibility of growth. Without the dissolution of each moment, you could never enjoy anything new.

Of course, the tendency is to resist the reality of change when things are to your liking. You've got everything just as it should be—the dishes are all done, the checkbook is balanced, the leaves are raked, the baby's diaper is changed—and you want it all to stay that way. But you're doomed to disappointment if you cling to any given moment, for time marches on, heedless of your objections.

Shiva is depicted as the one consciousness that looks out of every set of eyes in all worlds. He's the eternal witness to the parade of change, permanently lodged in meditative equipoise (balanced mind), unruffled by the shifting nature of phenomena. When you chant AUM NAMAH SHIVAYA, you're aligning your mind with your deepest core as that formless solitary observer—and because you're no longer mindlessly clinging or reactive, you can weather life's changing fortunes with stability and grace. More than this, you're equipped to welcome the reality of impermanence with gratitude. You can be sincerely thankful for the transformational possibilities of the destroying principle, the cosmic recycler.

5. Invoking the Supreme Form *(Durga)*

AUM AING HRING KLEENG
CHAMUNDAYE VICHCHEY AUM
SHREE DURGA MA NAMO NAMAH

AUM. Seed syllables of Saraswati (Wisdom),
Lakshmi/Parvati (Purification), and Kali (Transformation).
She who cuts off inappropriate aversion and attachment.
Revered Mother, Durga, I bow to you again and again.

In contrast to the masculine aspect of the Divine (the formless observer, epitomized by Lord Shiva), the Mother is all form. She's everything that can be observed. The Goddess is pure *shakti* (from the Sanskrit *shak,* meaning "potency" or "power"), the energy out of which the entire universe is composed. She is *mātā* (mother), the raw *material* that makes up all things. (Indeed, it's no accident that the related Latin word, *mater,* is the common root for the English words *matter* and *mother.*) Modern physics agrees: From the subatomic perspective, all matter, regardless of how solid it seems, is composed of pure energy. The only factor that keeps everything from falling through everything else is the relatively stable nature of the relationships among those whirling particles of energy.

Durga

The Mother assumes all forms—both the things you like and those you despise. She is life and death, prosperity and famine, health and disease. It's all her, including the body that you're borrowing to act out her desires. There's nowhere you can turn away from her, because even the head you're turning is made of Ma! The more of the world you can recognize as transparent to Deity, the more unbroken your communion with her will be. She'll meet you in anything and everything you can experience as Divine.

Chanting her mantra, your understanding is refined, and you realize that the Mother composes everything—there is no other. Deepening your devotion permits you to more readily distinguish her beneath the disguise she happens to be wearing, until finally she winks at you from within even the most hateful things. Developing this ability to see her in the unlikeliest of places and people makes it possible for you to cope with the inevitable difficulties of your life.

In addition to her identity as the substance of material reality, Durga is understood to be the Divine protector. Riding astride her terrifying mount, the lion Mrigaraj, she is the emblem of the ferociousness with which a mother defends her offspring. She'll take away your fear by helping you see that there's nowhere you could possibly go that would be even one atom's distance from her.

And what is it that she protects us *from?* She attacks our own self-centered orientation to life, expressed in clinging on the one hand and hatred on the other. These are the mechanisms we use to defend our illusory notions of our permanent and separate selves. We try to prop up the sand castle of ego by attaching ourselves to favored objects, ideas, causes, personalities, and events, while rejecting others that we don't like. But the Mother rushes in like the tide, obliterating the flimsy structure we've built to shield us from the twin realities of impermanence and interdependence.

6. Magnifying Self-Giving Love *(Jai Shree Devi)*

JAI SHREE DEVI NAMO NAMAH
Hooray for the Feminine Glory, the Goddess!
I bow to you again and again.

Our biological mothers fed us inside their wombs and then upon their breasts, giving us form and shaping us on every level thereafter. Our great mother, the earth, sustains us,

Standing Tara

often despite our heedless and harmful treatment of her. This is the defining quality of a mother's love: She selflessly cares for her own, sometimes even at great cost to herself.

Think of the times when your own mother spent herself for you. Maybe she suffered sleepless nights on your behalf while you were ill or went without so that you could have something special. The self-giving nature of maternal affection is rooted in seeing the loved one as equally important to—perhaps even more valuable than—yourself.

Among Tibetan Buddhists there's a spiritual exercise where you imagine that every individual you have ever encountered or will meet in the future is literally your own mother. They reason that since all sentient beings have gone through so many rebirths, each person must surely have been everyone else's mother at least once. One of the purposes for such an exercise is to cultivate the same sort of automatically caring, loyal response that you might have for your own beloved mother. When your heart is enlarged through this practice, you're empowered to broadcast that response to each and every being you encounter. Chanting this mantra will support you in recognizing the Divine Mother in all beings and in manifesting her extravagant care to everyone, without partiality or thought for personal reward.

7. Expanding Compassion
(Chenrezig)

AUM MANI PADME HUNG
AUM. The Jewel is in the Lotus!

These six syllables are so deeply in-grained in Tibetan folk consciousness that it's been called their national mantra. In-voking Avalokiteshvara (called Chenrezig in Tibetan)—the bodhisattva of compas-sion and patron deity of Tibet—the mantra begins (as do so many) with *AUM* and ends with *HUNG*, a kind of sonic exclamation point that discharges its energy. In between you'll find two words: *mani*, jewel; and *padme*, lotus—"the jewel is in the lotus."

The jewel is understood to represent indestructible bliss and emptiness. And where does this gem reside? In the lotus, representing the human condition. It grows in the swamp, right in the muck and mire,

127

yet it blooms forth in surpassing beauty, bridging Earth and heaven. Moreover, the lotus actually purifies its environment by growing there. Isn't this a vivid portrayal of our situation as human beings?

You may suppose that you comprehend bliss, as if it were simply amplified joy, but this isn't the case. Happiness is conditional; it depends on something sufficiently pleasant happening. Bliss, by contrast, is *un*conditional; it's the natural state of the radiant awareness that you always already are. Therefore, it can coexist with even the most sorrowful situations. Someone who's in authentic bliss has the ability to witness all situations—happy or sad—without inappropriately clinging to or discarding them. Rather, such a person accepts what appears with love, knowing that it's all part of the passing show.

The emptiness mentioned in this mantra is not the "bad news" emptiness of your mundane experience—empty bank account, empty refrigerator, empty gas tank, empty heart. Instead, as you discovered in Chapter 5, it describes the fact that all things lack independent existence. Everything is the result of a complex web of contributing factors, both material and subtle, including the labels and concepts that you use to make sense of it all. And this is no less true of yourself than it is of anything that you experience "out there." No thing has given rise to itself; each is interdependent with all.

Avalokiteshvara

Uniting these two insights, you can observe this completely connected array (of which you, too, are a part) from an ecstatic yet peaceful perspective. It's appropriate for you to be filled with wonder and gratitude at the mystery of it all. Chanting this mantra, you remind yourself that you—and all sentient beings—have the very seed of Divinity within yourself. No matter how distracted or confused you may become, your essential nature is pure, knowing, and luminous. It's this inherent absolute reality that you access, engage, and radiate when you forget yourself in chanting.

This mantra expands compassion both inwardly and outwardly. It invites you to realize that you're infinitely lovable and valuable, because you contain the ultimate treasure—and so does every other being you encounter!

8. Invoking Healing Energy *(Medicine Buddha)*

**TAYATA AUM BEKANZA BEKANZA
MAHA BEKANZA RANZE
SAMOGATE SOHA**
*This is how it is. AUM. Healing, healing,
Great Noble Healing within,
Permeate everywhere. So be it!*

Medicine Buddha

The Medicine Buddha represents the innate intelligence that maintains the health and wholeness of every living system. In the case of your physical body, this includes your immune system and regenerative powers. More subtle aspects of your being, such as your mental and emotional health, are preserved by your basic sanity, care, and openness. The Medicine Buddha personifies these healing processes and energies that support your well-being and ultimate realization.

Even the most staunch materialists in the medical profession acknowledge the importance of the patient's positive attitude. Meditating upon the Medicine Buddha cultivates a frame of mind conducive to healing, but goes beyond this to foster your own potential as a healer. The mantra implicates the person speaking or singing it in the transmission of therapeutic energies and practices.

As you chant this mantra, visualize the Medicine Buddha seated on a lotus about six inches above the crown of your head. He's blue in color because his nature is expansive like the sky or sea. He holds a golden bowl filled with *amrita,* the nectar of immortality, which takes the form of whatever medicine you happen to need in order to become healthy and whole in every dimension of your being. His eyes flutter open, and he inverts his bowl . . . a stream of nectar flows through your crown, down your central channel, through your throat, and finally fills your heart. Now blue light radiates in all directions from your core, curing all beings everywhere of whatever ails them in body, mind, and spirit.

9. Surrendering to Beauty *(Krishna)*

GOPALA GOVINDA GOVINDA GOPALA
DEVAKINANDANA GOPALA
Master of the Cows, Protector.
Joyful Shining God, Son of the Goddess.

During his days as a young cowherd, Krishna was reputed to have been the very Perfection of beauty. He magnetized everyone who saw him and inspired them to adoration. He's the all-attractive one, the quintessential object of desire.

Like the Medicine Buddha, Krishna is depicted as having blue skin. He's frequently shown holding a flute with which he charmed the *gopis* (cowherd girls). The stories of his love play with Radha (his favorite among the gopis) are commonly taken to epitomize the ideal relationship between the human soul and the Supreme.

Like me, you may regard traditional depictions of Krishna with indifference—you may not respond to this particular image as representing your notion of perfect beauty personified—and that's just fine. I encourage you to use your mind's eye and fix your inner gaze upon whatever holds ultimate fascination for you. What's powerfully attractive to me may not exert any pull on you at all. But each of us can usefully identify that special someone or something that answers to our need for our own personal Krishna.

Once upon a time there was a woman who tried a number of spiritual practices that promised enlightenment, but she never found one engaging enough that she could persevere in it. Disgruntled, she made her way to yet another teacher and asked what she might do to realize God.

He asked, "Is there anyone in your life whom you love?"

She replied, "Well, I have a nephew I'm rather fond of."

The teacher charged her: "From now on, you must see your nephew as Krishna. Worship him every day with offerings and chanting, lavishing your love upon him in every way you can."

The story goes that the woman was illuminated. And we can only imagine what a remarkable effect her love had upon her nephew-Krishna!

Krishna

Once you identify the person or thing you love best, you may realize that your attraction is rooted in your beloved's likeness to the Supreme. I recommend letting this thing or person be Divine in your own eyes; serve the affection that you feel with all of the intensity you can muster. You'll find that by exercising your love in this way, you're able to readily care for more of the world.

10. Energizing Yourself with the Life Force
(Green Tara)

AUM TARE TUTARE TURE SOHA
AUM. Homage to Tara, swift heroine, whose mantra Tutare dispels all fear, and Ture, which fulfills all needs.

Green Tara personifies the energy that animates living beings. She's lush green like fresh shoots of grass at the height of spring. She symbolizes the relentless quality of life: emerging and reemerging, no matter how wounded or barren the environment. Like those tendrils of plants whose heartiness defies all odds by breaking up through the asphalt on a summer day, Green Tara is the irrepressible life force.

Green Tara

She represents fertility, the fruition of the creative process, in all domains of life. She's the possibility of rejuvenation, of hope in the face of despair, and especially of courage despite all fears. Her mantra enables you to resonate with the subtle energies of renewal and encouragement.

We all find ourselves spent from time to time, exhausted from the struggle of *samsara,* the unceasing wheel of existence. Green Tara is a loving mother, providing solace and sustenance for the world-weary. Chanting her mantra, you'll find vigor, courage, and inspiration.

11. Decontaminating Yourself *(Vajrasattva)*

AUM VAJRASATTVA AUM AH HUNG
AUM. Indestructible Being,
purify my body, speech, and mind.

Vajrasattva, the essence of all awakened ones, represents the permanence and excellence of your nature as Radiant Awareness. Like a diamond (Sanskrit: *vajra*), your luminous, knowing essence is shatterproof. No matter how confused, deluded, or distracted you may become, your pristine awareness remains clear and whole. What's unconditionally real can't be corrupted.

Vajrasattva

Traditionally, the practice associated with Vajrasattva is designed to give you a fresh start. He's the purifying deity, burning away all of the negativities and obstructions from your body, speech, and mind. The accumulated residue of poor choices—affecting your physical, mental, emotional, relational, and spiritual lives—results in obstacles that delay or even thwart your progress. Your entire being is refined by presenting yourself for decontamination to the archetype of your own enlightened essence. You need to do this over and over again, always with an attitude of ruthlessly honest reflection. Consider this mantra a regular cleansing for misconduct (negative actions), misspeaking (ignorant and unkind talk), and misthinking (misperception and misinterpretation).

We're especially in need of purification for our failures in integrity: when we're untrue to ourselves. Vajrasattva is who we are underneath all of the façades, games, defenses, attachments, and aversions—when all our cases of mistaken identity are finally put to rest.

Here's the traditional visualization that's associated with Vajrasattva. (The relationship of the sites in the body to the dimensions of your being may seem unfamiliar, but this is how practitioners have performed this for many centuries.) When chanting this mantra, imagine Vajrasattva seated before you, facing you as if in a mirror that reflects your own image, but in a fully perfected form. At his forehead, he has an AUM radiating white light; at his throat, an AH glowing red; at his heart, a HUNG emanating blue light. These colored lights represent the transmission of Vajrasattva's unstained virtues and abilities to you.

Each time you come to the second AUM in the mantra, visualize the white light streaming from his forehead to your own, burning away all the negativities and obstructions from your body; with each AH, red light shoots from his throat to yours, cleansing away all impurities of your speech; with each HUNG, blue light radiates from his heart to yours, dissolving every pollution of your mind. What's left after this total de-contamination? Only your indestructible essence.

12. Dedicating Your Activities *(Karmapa)*

KARMAPA CHENNO
Source of all awakened activities, remember me.

Within the Tibetan Buddhist tradition, it's been long understood that certain extraordinary teachers come back, lifetime after lifetime, to help us progress on the path to enlightenment. The first person to be officially recognized as a reincarnated teacher was Düsum Khyenpa (1110–1193), after whom came a succession of individuals who have borne the title *Karmapa,* "source of awakened activity." Up to the present day, it's believed that this same being has returned 16 more times to inspire and equip his contemporaries in each generation for enlightenment.

While you may not put much stock in the notion of reincarnation, it's still reassuring to think that there are some people alive today who exemplify Radiant Awareness and Care. They serve as living "lights at the end of the tunnel," testifying to the possibility of awakening that's inherent in you. Because of their insight and great compassion, their example and instruction can guide you to that farther shore beyond the torrent of your own selfishness and confusion.

The Karmapa principle is simple: There are beings who demonstrate the achievability of your own highest goal-state; they're not limited to the mythic past. If you're fortunate enough to discover them, you may call out to them—if only in your imagination: *Remember me!* You're asking a pioneer of liberation to continue leading you toward your awakened destiny—one choice, one action, at a time. In this circuit of

His Holiness 17th Gyalwang Karmapa, Ogyen Trinley Dorje.

remembrance, you remember to remind your ideal to recollect you. You fix your mind upon your source of inspiration and imagine that they're just as focused on you. Identifying with your "Karmapa" in this way is like putting a deposit on your fruition to a life of true freedom, unfettered by ignorance, hatred, and grasping.

13. Requesting Realization *(Guru Rinpoche)*

AUM AH HUNG VAJRA GURU PADME SIDDHI HUNG

Indestructible remover of darkness,
Please purify my body, speech, and mind,
And grant me ordinary and supreme realization.

This mantra to Guru Rinpoche ("precious remover of darkness") is traditionally associated with Padmasambhava, the 8th-century *mahasiddha* ("foremost spiritual practitioner") who brought Buddha's teaching from India to Tibet. Celebrated for his supernatural contests with fierce local deities, Padmasambhava went beyond merely subduing them. He didn't destroy or expel them, instead converting them into "dharma

Padmasambhava

protectors," mighty beings who use their considerable powers to defend the path of illumination—and those who traverse it—from all enemies.

You, too, must hand over the demonic aspects of your self-structure to your remover of darkness for transformation into something positive. These shadow-aspects are the residue of faulty parenting, unhealed abuse, unforgiven injuries, and hidden pockets of selfishness. You must acknowledge your shadow, not deny or repress it. Only by bringing these things to light can they be converted into servants of awakening.

After intoning the syllables that purify body, speech, and mind (see Chant 11), you ask your imperishable guru—the enlightened one who removes the darkness of ignorance—to provide you with ordinary and supreme realization. The achievement of *ordinary* realization implies success and well-being in your mundane life (which creates a climate that supports dedicated spiritual practice). *Supreme* realization, in contrast, is enlightenment itself, which dissolves the painful (although commonplace) delusion that you're separate and limited.

14. Learning Your Life Lessons *(Saturn)*

AUM SHAM SHANISH CHARIYA NAMAHA
AUM. I bow down to Lord Saturn (the Slow-Mover).

Since ancient times, astrologers the world over have understood that the positions of the sun, moon, and planets as they move relative to Earth seem to coordinate with specific events that may be observed in the lives of human beings. These effects are so regular that the various celestial bodies were treated as distinct personalities (a practice echoed, for example, in the ancient Roman pantheon: Jupiter, king of the gods; Mars, god of war; and Venus, goddess of love and beauty).

Saturn, the "slow-mover" (taking nearly 30 years to complete one circuit through the constellations), is depicted as an elderly teacher. He's a strict disciplinarian who insists that you learn your life lessons—even the hard way, if need be. He's your tireless tutor, demanding that you master yourself through self-control.

Saturn (whose mandala is depicted on the next page) is associated with *karma,* the inevitable linkage between cause and effect. As such, he represents the inescapability of the consequences of your choices in life. Under Saturn's influence, your

Saturn Mandala

karmas ripen rapidly so that the ramifications of your actions are made manifest. He also represents those forces governing your life that you neither comprehend nor control, but which nevertheless affect you.

Offering salutations to Saturn through this mantra implies your submission to the discipline of cause and effect. You're agreeing to pay close attention to life's lessons about the quality of the choices you make and to adopt an attitude of surrender rather than rebellion when the universe seems to be opposing you. This mantra helps cultivate a sense of personal accountability for the results you're getting, in the place of your customary—and sometimes futile—resistance when things aren't to your liking. You can then more readily digest your disappointments and grow both in grace and responsibility.

This rich heritage of mantras is now yours to chant. Speak and sing them into the depths of your heart and mind so that they can illuminate the dark corners of your being and upgrade your powers of thought, feeling, and action. In the Conclusion, you'll have the opportunity to consider the renewed vision available when you make chanting the cornerstone of your spiritual practice.

Conclusion

Making Your Life and World Divine Through Chant

Until recently, practical spiritual treasures such as devotional chanting were available only to religious professionals in their countries of origin. No prior generation has enjoyed our opportunities to access insights and solutions discovered and proven in far-flung corners of the world. And no people in history have stood in greater need of these tools for moving beyond the conventional limits of a self-grasping way of life. The cultural mixing that characterizes the present seems to call for such a method.

As my guru says, "Everybody's everywhere," so it's high time we began to genuinely learn from each other. Devotional chanting is a comprehensive system of spiritual exercise that simply fits us and the world we're living in.

Ironically, in this spiritual practice you learn to use sound to take you to silence. You're redirected toward the best that you can imagine through the ardent repetition of the supreme sound forms. Along the way, you acquire skills in managing your mind, heart, motivations, and relationships. As your practice matures, your ability to focus on, visualize, emulate, and identify with your ideals improves; you progressively out-grow your habitual dualism; and you come to finally abide in your essential nature as Radiant Awareness and Care.

The result of a daily devotional chanting regimen is new mental and emotional habits, which are organized around the supreme target of your attention and affection and are expressed in varied and beautiful sound forms. As you move through each moment, you may use the mantra most perti-nent to the demands of your present situation. Let the chants function as an internal soundtrack to your life, qualifying each experience with their invocations of Perfection.

Following sound into silence means working with man-tras—these timeless Perfections that you breathe into being—in order to discover and reside within the space between the breaths, between the sounds, between the thoughts. When you find yourself jammed up by a chaos of concerns, you need only refresh yourself in the ocean of devotion. Dive into the mantra wave that's always crashing on the shore of your awareness, thanks to your disciplined practice.

My guru says that the mind is like a tree, its limbs heavy with a massive flock of birds, each one representing a different thought or feeling. They're chirping and squawking at each other, creating a tumult that pushes inner peace out of reach. Chanting a mantra with devotion drives these birds away; then we can rest in the silence until they return—and they *will* return. But the promise of this practice is that, with dedicated effort, they'll stay away longer and come back in fewer numbers.

My guru also likens our interior life within this practice to a kind of shuttling back and forth between form (represented in the figure of Kali Ma, a fierce version of the Mother) and the formless (epitomized by Shiva, the Father). In devotional chanting, we scale down the quantity of thought-forms to one (the mantra), bringing analytical reasoning to a standstill. Then we dwell tranquilly in the formless silence for as long as we're able: "You stay with Father till Mother kicks you out!" As our practice deepens, our clarity and the duration of our serenity tend to increase.

Enlightenment is frequently represented as an instantaneous event. The illuminated person is depicted as permanently lodged in a serene condition, insulated from the frustrations and sufferings of everyday life. But what if this experience is something that's achieved one thought, one feeling, one action at a time? Maybe what appears to be a supernatural otherness on the part of the realizer is actually, from the inside, simply a succession of intelligent, loving choices so regular that it appears the person is immune from ordinary cares. If such beings give the impression of unshakable calm and infinite self-possession, I suggest that it's probably the result of stability of focus and devotion—something hard-won by steadfast spiritual practice. Such procedures provide an enduring ability to arrive at good decisions, each making the next easier, likelier, and more spontaneous.

You, too, can form habits conducive to realization. That's the precise purpose of devotional chanting. This mystical training empowers you to encounter every person, every situation, every moment, as transparent to Deity—meaning that you're eventually able to see the Divine through the mundane, including yourself. Chanting mantras doesn't magically transmute the reality you face—although it certainly seems so from the inside. The objects of your awareness and care aren't actually undergoing any change whatsoever. They remain what they've always been, but before investing in a chanting practice, you were probably too distracted in your perceptions and distorted in your interpretations to notice. All are manifestations of pure Spirit, assuming manifold forms according to the whim of the Divine Mother. It's you yourself who's undertaking transformation: Your vision is being corrected so that you can view the world with Supreme sight. It takes a Divinity to see and recognize the Divine; you're the eyes of the living universe looking upon itself with wonder, awe, acceptance, and love.

Devotional chanting prepares your mind to experience the world, and yourself in it, in the manner perhaps best expressed in mantras—or in the heights of mystic poetry, such as this passage from Walt Whitman (*Leaves of Grass:* "Song of Myself," stanza 48):

I hear and behold God in every object. . . .
I see something of God each hour of the twenty-four,
and each moment then;
In the faces of men and women I see God,
and in my own face in the glass;
I find letters from God dropt in the street—
and every one is sign'd by God's name,
And I leave them where they are, for I know that wheresoe'er I go,
Others will punctually come forever and ever.

When your mind and heart are saturated with mantras, you experience a world populated with gods and goddesses. Every nook and cranny is filled to bursting with the Perfections that you've equipped yourself to recognize. This is Divinization—the ability to perceive the Supreme in every moment. Always fresh from your revitalizing chanting practice, you'll never be at a loss for something to love. Nor will you find yourself short of affection with which to embrace these other parts of yourself.

Concluding Mantra

156

I believe that it's appropriate to close with a mantra—this one is among the simplest that I know, but also among the most powerful.

15. Reuniting Yourself with the Divine *(Sita Ram)*

**RAMA RAMA RAMA RAMA RAMA
SITA RAM SITA RAM SITA RAM JAYA SITA RAM**
Incarnate Preserving Deity,
Hooray for the Union of Our Soul with the Supreme!

Rama & Sita

This was the mantra of Hanuman, the Divine monkey, as well as that of my guru's guru, Neem Karoli Baba, who was regarded as a manifestation of Hanuman. He chanted "Ram" day and night for more than 40 years. He even spent a year and a half standing in a lake, up to his neck in the water, chewing over his "Rams." Maharaji, as he was called by his devotees, kept a daily journal in which he recorded his appointments and important ideas. When some of his more inquisitive students stole a peek at it, they saw that each entry began with the date, followed by line after line, page after page, of nothing but "Ram," written neatly over and over again. It's safe to say that Neem Karoli had Ram on his mind!

In the Indian epic the *Ramayana,* crown prince Ram—an incarnation of the god of preservation, Vishnu—was about to be enthroned as king in his father's stead. But through envious intrigue in his family, he was banished into the wilderness for 14 years, accompanied by his brother, Lakshman, and his wife, Sita, reputed to be the most beautiful woman in all the worlds. During their exile, the demon-king of Lanka, Ravana, having learned of Sita's beauty and wanting her for himself, kidnapped her and stole her away to his palace. Even though Ram was an incarnation of the great god Vishnu, he needed help to recover Sita. Of all those who came to his aid, Hanuman was most instrumental in reuniting the Divine couple.

(An incarnation of Shiva, Hanuman—known as the son of the wind—was capable of amazing feats of strength, such as leaping to the sun in his youth, jumping across the ocean, and picking up a mountain in one hand. When Ram asked Hanuman how he was able to perform such exploits, Hanuman answered that it was because he always had Ram's name upon his lips!)

An allegorical interpretation of this story identifies Ram as God, Sita as our own soul, Ravana as our ego-clinging tendency, and Hanuman as our breath, with which we chant the Divine name. Our very soul has been stolen away from God by our own selfishness. How are we to be reunited with the Divine? By combining our breath with the name of God. We forget ourselves in the very act of passionately remembering our ideal. In chanting this mantra, we unite ourselves (Sita) with the Supreme (Ram).

Let's chant: RAMA RAMA RAMA RAMA RAMA. . . .

Acknowledgments

Leading devotional chanting and *satsang* (Sanskrit for "truth-gathering") was not a career to which I aspired before meeting the man who was to become my guru, Bhagavan Das. During his six-year sojourn on the Indian Subcontinent, Baba was an ardent student of many spiritual practices across several wisdom traditions, preeminently devotional chanting. Many Westerners' first exposure to Sanskrit-based chanting came through his performances and recordings. When he initiated me, Baba opened my heart in a way I had never before experienced. He named me after Mount Kailash, in the Himalayan range of western Tibet—considered the sacred symbolic center of the world within the Hindu, Buddhist, and Bonpo traditions. It's my hope to emulate and to transmit Baba's inspiring example of devotion, for the benefit of all beings.

Before we met, my friend (psychic medium) John Holland heard me giving a chanting demonstration at an open house hosted by a mutual friend. I was explaining that in repeating the mantras we can "follow the sound into silence." That little phrase stuck with him, and he told the president of Hay House (his publisher and now mine) about it. This book is the result of conversations sparked by John's suggestion, for which I am most grateful.

I also owe a debt of gratitude to the many folks who have chanted with me at numerous kirtan events over these past few years. Sharing this practice with them has helped me explore and understand devotional chanting far more deeply than I could ever have done on my own.

My own *dakini*, Jaishree, is far more to me than any conventional role—wife, best friend, editor, partner—can imply. She defines devotion in her treatment of our son and me. I am blessed to have this goddess at the center of my life.

Resources

The following Websites and books provide information to help you get started learning about deities the world over.

Websites

http://www.lowchensaustralia.com/names/gods.htm
http://www.godchecker.com
http://en.wikipedia.org/wiki/List_of_deities
http://ancienthistory.about.com/library/bl/bl_myth_gods_index.htm
http://www.beliefnet.com/index.html?rnd=639

Books

Eric Chaline, *The Book of Gods & Goddesses: A Visual Directory of Ancient & Modern Deities* (New York: Quid Publishing, 2004).

Alain Daniélou, *The Myths and Gods of India: The Classic Work on Hindu Polytheism* (Rochester, Vermont: Inner Traditions, 1991).

Elizabeth Hallam, ed., *Gods and Goddesses: A Treasury of Deities and Tales from World Mythology* (New York: Macmillan, 1996).

Manfred Lurker, *A Dictionary of Gods and Goddesses, Devils and Demons* (Oxford, U.K.: Routledge, 1987).

Philip Wilkinson, *Illustrated Dictionary of Religions: Figures, Festivals, and Beliefs of the World's Religions* (New York: Penguin Books, Ltd., 1999).

About the Author

Kailash is committed to sharing tools of mind, heart, speech, and song that equip practitioners for success in the search for happiness. For many years a scholar-teacher in human communication and psychology (as Kurt A. Bruder, Ph.D., M.Ed.) and an earnest student of spirituality, Kailash presents a unique blend of wisdom and inspiration useful to those on any path to the Supreme.

Kailash lives with his beloved wife, Jaishree, and their son, Bodhi Shankara, near Asheville, North Carolina. He regularly facilitates devotional chanting events and offers instruction in spiritually relevant themes. For more information about Kailash, a schedule of his appearances, and other material of potential interest, please visit his Website at: **http://OmKailash.com**.

Mantras with Translation
Good Medicine for Your Heart and Mind

1. The All-Inclusive Mantra
   AUM

2. Beginning Well *(Ganesha)*
   AUM GANG GANAPATAYE NAMAHA SWAHA
   GANG GANAPATAYE NAMO NAMAH
   GANESHA SHARANAM JAI JAI GANESHA
   AUM. I bow to Ganesha (Lord of Categories). So be it!
   GANG (Ganesha's signature sound). I bow to Ganesha
   again and again.
   I take refuge in Ganesha. Hooray, hooray for Ganesha!

3. Changing Your Trajectory *(Saman Mantra)*
   ASATO MA SAT GAMAYA
   TAMASO MA JYOTIR GAMAYA
   MRITYOR MA AMRITAM GAMAYA
   AUM SHANTI SHANTI SHANTIHI
   Lead us from the unreal to the Real,
   From darkness to Light,
   From death to Immortality.
   AUM. Peace, peace, peace be upon us all.

4. Invoking the Formless Supreme *(Shiva)*
   AUM NAMAH SHIVAYA
   AUM. I bow down to Shiva (The Auspicious One).

5. Invoking the Supreme Form *(Durga)*
   **AUM AING HRING KLEENG CHAMUNDAYE
   VICHCHEY AUM**
   *AUM. Seed syllables of Saraswati (Wisdom), Lakshmi/Parvati
   (Purification), and Kali (Transformation). She who cuts off
   inappropriate aversion and attachment.*

6. Magnifying Self-Giving Love *(Jai Shree Devi)*
   JAI SHREE DEVI NAMO NAMAH
   *Hooray for the Feminine Glory, the Goddess!
   I bow to you again and again.*

7. Expanding Compassion *(Chenrezig)*
   AUM MANI PADME HUNG
   AUM. The Jewel is in the Lotus!

8. Invoking Healing Energy *(Medicine Buddha)*
   **TAYATA AUM BEKANZA BEKANZA
   MAHA BEKANZA RANZE
   SAMOGATE SOHA**
   *This is how it is. AUM. Healing, healing,
   Great Noble Healing within,
   Permeate everywhere. So be it!*

9. Surrendering to Beauty *(Krishna)*
   **GOPALA GOVINDA GOVINDA GOPALA
   DEVAKINANDANA GOPALA**
   *Master of the Cows, Protector.
   Joyful Shining God, Son of the Goddess.*

10. Energizing Yourself with the Life-Force *(Green Tara)*
   AUM TARE TUTARE TURE SOHA
   *AUM. Homage to Tara, swift heroine, whose mantra Tutare
   dispels all fear, and Ture, which fulfills all needs.*

11. Decontaminating Yourself *(Vajrasattva)*
   AUM VAJRASATTVA AUM AH HUNG
   AUM. Indestructible Being, purify my body, speech, and mind.

12. Dedicating Your Activities *(Karmapa)*
   KARMAPA CHENNO
   Source of all awakened activities, remember me.

13. Requesting Realization *(Guru Rinpoche)*
   AUM AH HUNG VAJRA GURU PADME SIDDHI HUNG
   *Indestructible remover of darkness,
   Please purify my body, speech, and mind,
   And grant me ordinary and supreme realization.*

14. Learning Your Life-Lessons *(Saturn)*
   AUM SHAM SHANISH CHARIYA NAMAHA
   AUM. I bow down to Lord Saturn (The Slow-Mover).

15. Reuniting Yourself with the Divine *(Sita Ram)*
   **RAMA RAMA RAMA RAMA RAMA
   SITA RAM SITA RAM SITA RAM JAYA SITA RAM**
   *Incarnate Preserving Deity,
   Hooray for the Union of Our Soul with the Supreme!*

All songs written by Kurt "Kailash" Bruder BMI © 2007, Sonny Salinas ASCAP © 2007, Jim Wyse BMI © 2007

Musicians: Kurt "Kailash" Bruder: Vocals, Ektaras / Sonny Salinas: Drums, electric guitars, keyboards, loops, and percussion / Tyler Ramsey: Acoustic guitars, Hammond B-3, and Moog Voyager / Bill Reynolds: Bass guitar / Jim Wyse: Acoustic guitar on "Shiva"

Recorded at Echo Mountain Recording, Asheville, North Carolina. Additional recording at Whitewater Studios, Asheville, North Carolina, and Hay House Radio Studios. *Engineered by:* Julian Dreyer / *Assistant engineer:* Jon Ashley / *Mixed by:* Sonny Salinas at Hay House Radio Studios and Christian Haene at Mazzive Sound Studios, Beil, Switzerland / *Mastered by:* Serge Christen at Mazzive Sound Studios

Ganesha by Bhagavan Das: adapted by Kurt Bruder, Sonny Salinas / *Shiva* by Bhagavan Das: adapted by Kurt Bruder, James Wyse, Sonny Salinas / *Medicine Buddha* by Jean Philippe Rykiel and Lama Gyurme: adapted by Kurt Bruder, Sonny Salinas / *Krishna* (Devakinandana Gopala) by Dave Stringer: adapted by Kurt Bruder / *Sita Ram* by Bhagavan Das: adapted by Kurt Bruder

Notes

Notes

Notes

Notes